The

Twin

Towers

Trilogy

Sal Umana

The Twin Towers Trilogy

A Spirituality for the Age of Terrorism

THE TWIN TOWERS TRILOGY

The Twin Towers Trilogy
A Spirituality for the Age of Terrorism

Book One

The Day God Died
How the Twin Towers Became the Grave of the God of Monotheism

Book Two

The Day My Ego Died
How the Twin Towers on 9/11/01 Became the Grave of My Ego

Book Three

Back To Earth
Living and Dying Without Ego

The Twin Towers Trilogy
A Spirituality for the Age of Terrorism

Book One

The Day God Died, is about the Twin Towers becoming
the Grave of the Personal God We Grew Up With.

Book Two

The Day My Ego Died, is about the death of our personal Ego and
Life as Love, or living for the Other because he or she is me.

Book Three

Back To Earth, is about dying each moment and living
each moment as part of the Oneness of Being

CONTENTS

BOOK 1 THE DAY GOD DIED

BOOK 2 THE DAY MY EGO DIED

THE TWIN TOWERS TRILOGY

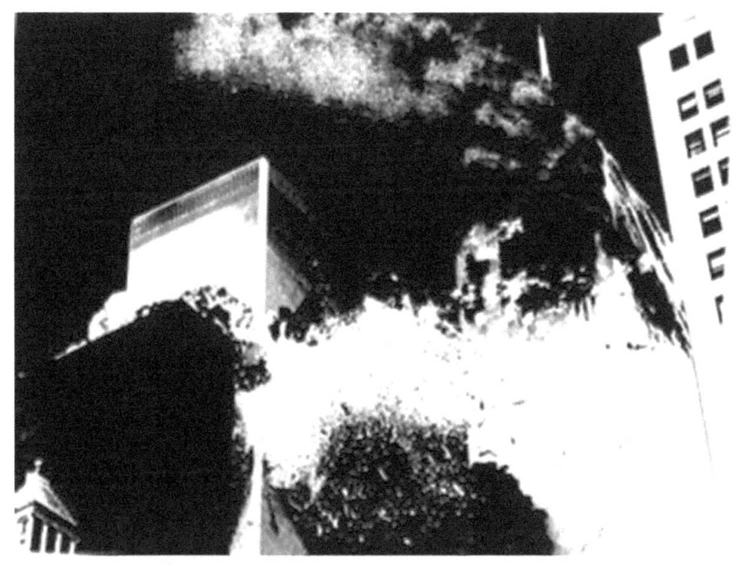

A SPIRITUALITY FOR THE AGE OF TERRORISM

Preface to this Trilogy

FOR THE TENTH anniversary of 9/11, I decided to write the third book that I had promised at the end of my second book. The third book was going to be a "Better World" Retreat to the General Assembly of the United Nations, preached by me as a member of the non-governmental organization at the UN called "The Movement for a Better World." In this retreat, I was going to call upon all the nations of the world to become "The United States of the World." With my spirituality of the Oneness of Being, it was going to be a no-brainer. But the no-brainer turned out to be my Ego.

When the Bush Administration and their neo-conservative Imperialists declared "preventive war" on the Muslim World, and rushed our willing young lads into Afghanistan, and then into Iraq, and planned several proxy attacks on Iran, they completely broke what was left of my heart, and I abandoned that presumptuous fantasy effort at the UN. It was going to take a while till the phony "War On Terror" was settled by a loving truce with everyone in the world who either hated or envied the U.S.'s greedy Ego trip with the world.

So ten years later, I have decided to publish a Trilogy called "The Twin Towers Trilogy". In it will be the first book I wrote: "The Day God Died: How the Twin Towers Became the Grave of the God of Monotheism", and the second book, "The Day My Ego Died: How The Twin towers Became the Grave of My Ego." They are being republished in a new volume with the third book: "Back To Earth: A Spirituality For the Age of Terrorism."

Ten years ago I startled some people when I wrote about God coming to me with a nervous breakdown and an identity crisis, and also suffering from Post Traumatic Stress Disorder. People don't like to hear about Almighty God having a nervous breakdown. I, myself, with my then inflated Ego, was ill-prepared for such a complicated patient as God, despite thirty years of experience as a psychotherapist. Especially since I no longer really believed in a personal God like God Almighty, the Father in Heaven, whose name is very hallowed. You see, both God and I had one of the most traumatic experiences of our lives. It was September 11, 2001, and God is a New Yorker (what else?), and I am a New Yorker. When the two of us saw the Twin Towers go down in smoke and fire, we were not only mortally, irreversibly traumatized, but we were scared as Hell, because we knew intuitively that the Third Milennium was not going to be a comfortable ride through space.

Well, it turns out that God who came to me for therapy was an internalized projection of divinity. What that means, I am about to tell you. You see, this God was a figment of my imagination, and for thirty years I had been trying to figure out what the real God was all about, if there was One. So I graciously, sometimes not so graciously, did a course of psychotherapy on my idea of God. Well, all heaven broke loose, and God and I had huge fights, and She went through a massive identity crisis, and turned out to be a thirteen billion year old teenager, (yes, a teenager in cosmic years), and completely renounced all human ideas of God to the extent that She became a full-blown atheist!

Well, it all ended up okay because I sang a paean of praise to "Whatever God" calling her whatever is cuddly, adorable, and magnificent in the universe, ending up with naming Her the One, the True, the Good, the Beautiful, and finally, Love Itself.

We don't know if God fell for this, but a year later, I went to Her and asked Her to do a course of therapy on me, basically, to return the favor After an hour of shouting and screaming at each other, God reluctantly took me on as a patient. But she refused to accept Medicare, because we tried that with Her therapy, and Medicare would not hear of it. I am sure that I was one of the most impatient patients she ever treated.

It was in the course of this treatment that I was asked to commit Ego suicide for no reason whatsoever, except that God didn't have an Ego, so why should I? You don't understand? Then read the second book enclosed here.

All of this should have been enough, but along comes this tenth anniversary of the Twin Towers Tragedy, and after denouncing the war on terrorism as a fraud perpetrated on the U.S.A. by the military-industrial – complex and the American Imperialists, I see a team of Navy Seals gun down Osama Bin Laden and toss him in the Indian Ocean, and we are back to Judeo-Christian triumphalist revenge. So, as a member of Pax/Christi/USA, I had to write a third book on "Spirituality for the Age of Terrorism. " First I had to explain the "God Who Never Was" in the First Chapter, and the "God Who Always Was" in the second chapter. But God was relatively fine. It was my not quite dead Ego that needed the work. So I did a real time actual self-analysis with God as my imagined therapist, and as George Bush would say about his Buddy Brown, "She did a heck of a job." This I expanded on in the rest of the book, guiding the reader through the agony of the Dark Night of the Ego. We learned that the Ego does not exist in reality, but is a mental construct of the human brain that comes down to us through "survival of the fittest" Evolution. Suffice it to say that you have a trip before you that could be a little rockier than *Eat, Pray, Love*, namely, Die to your old ideas about God, die to your Ego, and Die. Period.

But, hopefully, you will end up in the same place: *LOVE.*

As an old standard from my childhood sings:

> *"I'll be loving you, always, with a love that's true, always . . .*
> *"Not for just an hour, not for just a day, not for just a year,*
> *"But always."*

A Note on Spirituality

W E PROMISED THAT we would offer you "A Spirituality for the Age of Terrorism," but what exactly *is* "spirituality"? We need to clarify what we mean by "Spirituality".

Spirituality, like philosophy, means many different concepts to many different people. For the purposes of this Trilogy, I define spirituality as broadly as I can, with the hope of appealing to as many people as I possibly can. My fond hope is that my spiritual outlook on human existence is compatible with all human beings, regardless of religion, or regardless of political ideology, or lack of it. Regardless of whether they are theists or atheists, I hope to appeal to whatever philosophy the reader has been exposed to. Philosophy is, literally, "the love of wisdom", and concerns itself especially with the "ultimate facts and principles of reality and of human nature and conduct." (Webster's New Collegiate Dictionary, Merriam, Springfield, MA,1959)

The spirituality which I have lived for the past ten years may be called "new age" spirituality by those who feel a need to categorize where I am coming from, but it is hardly new in its basic elements and really goes back to the dawn of human consciousness, as I will explain in Chapter Two of the Third Book: "The God Who Always Was".

There are two basic forms of spirituality afoot in the world today: religious spirituality and secular spirituality. Religious spirituality is based on the faith, beliefs, and teachings of whatever religion one chooses to follow. Secular spirituality is based, not on a series of beliefs, held on faith, or taught by authority like religious spirituality, but on practice. I have said elsewhere that this is the difference between *orthodoxy* and *orthopraxy.* Orthodoxy is about "The Right Teachings" and orthopraxy is about "The Right Practices." Jesus' famous statement: "By their fruits you shall know them", says that you can tell who has the truth, not by what they say or teach, but by what they do, or how they act in practice.

Another way of putting it: If a spirituality, a way of thinking or non-thinking, or of being or of doing, leads you to love yourself (your true self, that is), and leads you to love all those around you, you are on the right track.

If the spirituality you embrace leads you to fear and guilt, and anxiety, you are on the wrong track.

If the spirituality you embrace leads you to joy, you are on the right track.

Recently, I encountered a book on spirituality that contains most of the ideas that I have in my books. The book is: *This Is It: Dialogues On the Nature of Oneness*, by Jan Kersschot, (Watkins Publishing, London, 2004). Jan Kersschot has an interview with Ekhart Tolle another great spiritual teacher, which says very beautifully what the spirituality I espouse is all about.

"Jan Kersschot: The story goes that you spent two years living on park benches before you started to talk about this.

"Ekhart T.: I was lost in Being. The present moment was so fulfilling that I had completely lost interest in the future. The future and all the rest didn't matter any more. I was in some sort of continuous state of joy. Sometimes my mind would come in and ask, 'How can you be so happy?'

"JT.: You got lost in Beingness?

"ET.: Yes. One aspect of the transformation that happened to me was that the stream of thinking became reduced considerably.

"JK.: You were walking around with very little thought?

"ET.: Yes. I was walking around with very little thought. Without realizing it.

"JK.: I see.

"ET.: The wonderful thing is to relate to the world and yourself without the screen of interpretation and conceptualization. So, not relating to yourself and others through mental noise but through stillness.

"JK.: That is what awakening means to you? "ET.: Yes: Knowing yourself to be the stillness. "JK.: At that time, you were so to speak lost in this stillness.

"ET.: But gradually I managed to function in the world again. I couldn't be sitting on a park bench in Russell Square for the rest of my life. I gradually regained the balance between being and doing."

This "reducing the amount of thinking", and cutting down on the "screen of mental noise" is one of the main tenets of zen meditation. I call it "teaching yourself not to think." This is one of the biggest stumbling blocks to our Ego, for Ego uses this "conceptualization and interpretation" constantly to take us away from the present moment and drive us into guilt about the past and anxiety about the future.

Jan Kersschot and Ekhart Tolle both teach a spirituality based, not on thinking but on being. To enter into the Oneness of Being, we don't have to do anything, or say anything, or think anything, we just have to BE what we already are: in the Oneness of Being, or Unicity, but they are all interchangeable terms for God, Allah, Brahman, the Dao. Neither Tolle or Ekhart embrace the teachings of the religions about God, Allah, or Brahman, but they are all talking about the same Universal Power of Being which Kersschott calls "IT." I prefer my description of "The God who always was" as synonymous with their "Beingness." I emphasize what Ekhart Tolle says about his thinking being diminished by 90 % since his experience of "Enlightenment", or "Awakening."

I relate to this diminishment of bad thinking, which Tolle calls The Pain-Body, the accumulation of guilt, regrets, anger, and anxiety flooding our minds and drowning our Ego/false-self in a sea of pain. With this diminishment of negative thoughts I have found peace and joy and, of course, compassion for my fellow man drowning in this sea of self-induced pain.

After a lifetime search for "enlightenment" or "awakening," I am finally coming to see it as acceptance of the reality that I am not an individual being, but I exist within the Oneness of Being. I am not part of the Oneness of Being, because if Being is One, it obviously has no parts. But my true spirit/self exists within the Oneness of Being, that is, in Beingness itself, as Kersschot and Tolle say. (If you want to hear this in terms understandable to Christian tradition: " In Him we live and move, and have our being." (St. Paul)

THE DAY GOD DIED

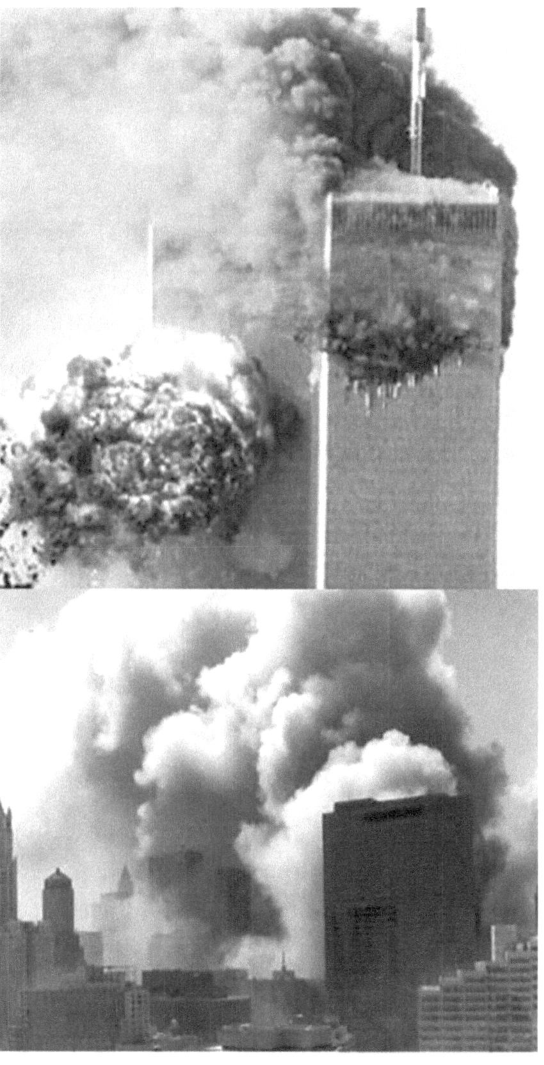

HOW THE TWIN TOWERS BECAME THE GRAVE
OF THE GOD OF MONOTHEISM

SAL UMANA

ON SEPTEMBER 11, 2001, the therapist-author imagines God coming to him for psychotherapy after the terrorist attacks and U.S. declaration of war on terrorists. God is appalled at the violence perpetrated by religious people on both sides, in His name, since He has always been completely opposed to such absurd and pointless barbarism.

Is God having a nervous breakdown, or just suffering from Post-Traumatic Stress Syndrome? From Sept. 11 to December 11, God comes for therapy once a week and in the course of treatment, discovers that She is having an Identity Crisis. She realizes that the old masculine tribal God of monotheism has been foisted on Her by the three great religions of the western world, while all spiritual people, both East and West have always experienced Her as Love. In a final surprise session, God tells the therapist who She really is and who we are.

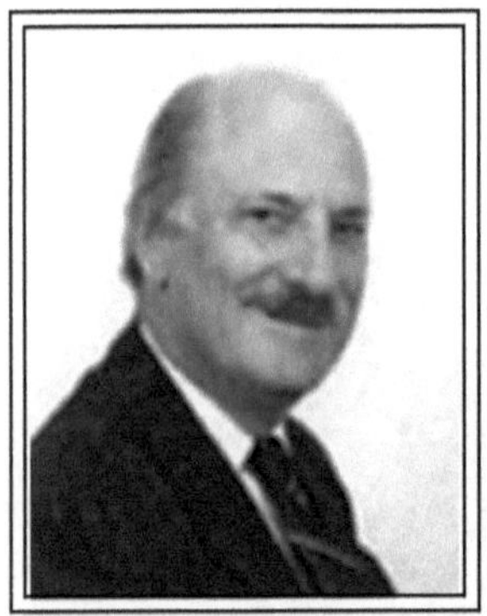

Sal Umana was born in South Boston, MA in 1929, the year of the Crash. He attended Boston Public Latin School, then became a Redemptorist Missionary and worked in all 50 states, the Caribbean, and Italy, for 25 years. He left the clerical priesthood to marry and for 25 more years, has practiced psychotherapy in New York as a Clinical Social Worker in English, Italian, and Spanish.

God has been his best patient. (She worked with him in English.)

THE DAY GOD DIED

THE DAY GOD DIED:

*How the Twin Towers Have Become the
Grave of the God of Monotheism*

BY SAL UMANA

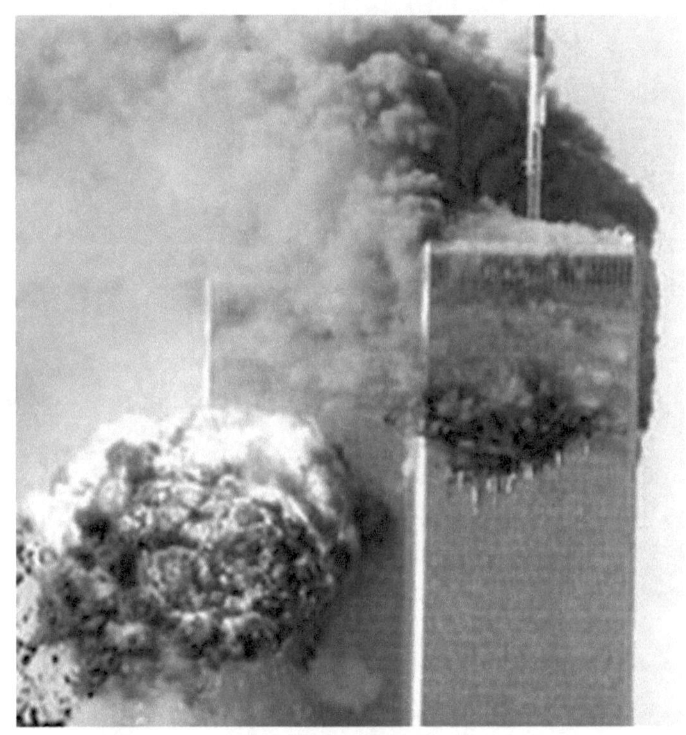

THE GRAVE OF THE GOD OF MONOTHEISM

To Jack Wilcox, who gave his life to make this a Better World, and whose ashes lie beneath his favorite tree at Genesis Farm, New Jersey,

And to my wife, Peggy, who actually read this book and liked it.

And finally, To Mary Ann and Ron Bastian in whose kitchen I saw the Towers collapse. But most of all to Ron, who drove me from California to New York

EPIGRAPH

And God said to me: Write:
     Leave the cruelty to kings.
      Without that angel
barring the way to love
     there would be no bridge for me into time.
And God said to me, Paint:
    Time is the canvas
    Stretched by my pain:
    The wounding of woman,
    The brothers' betrayal,
    The city's sad bacchanals,
    The madness of kings.
And God said to me, Go forth:
    For I am king of time.
    But to you I am only the shadowy one
    Who knows with you your loneliness
and sees through your eyes.
He sees through my eyes
In all the ages.
    And…
What will you do, God, when I die?
I am your pitcher (when I shatter?)
I am your drink (when I go bitter ?)
I, your garment; I, your craft.
Without me what reason have you?
What will you do, God ? I am afraid.

Rainer Maria Rilke

Acknowledgements

I WOULD LIKE TO thank everybody who has ever loved me, and thus revealed God to me.

I thank especially my wife, my parents, my sister and brothers, my relatives and friends.

I also acknowledge my teachers, who during twenty three years of school showed me by their concern who God was.

I thank my therapists who spoke directly to me from God- well, most of the time.

Finally, I thank my patients who taught me more than I could ever hope to teach them.

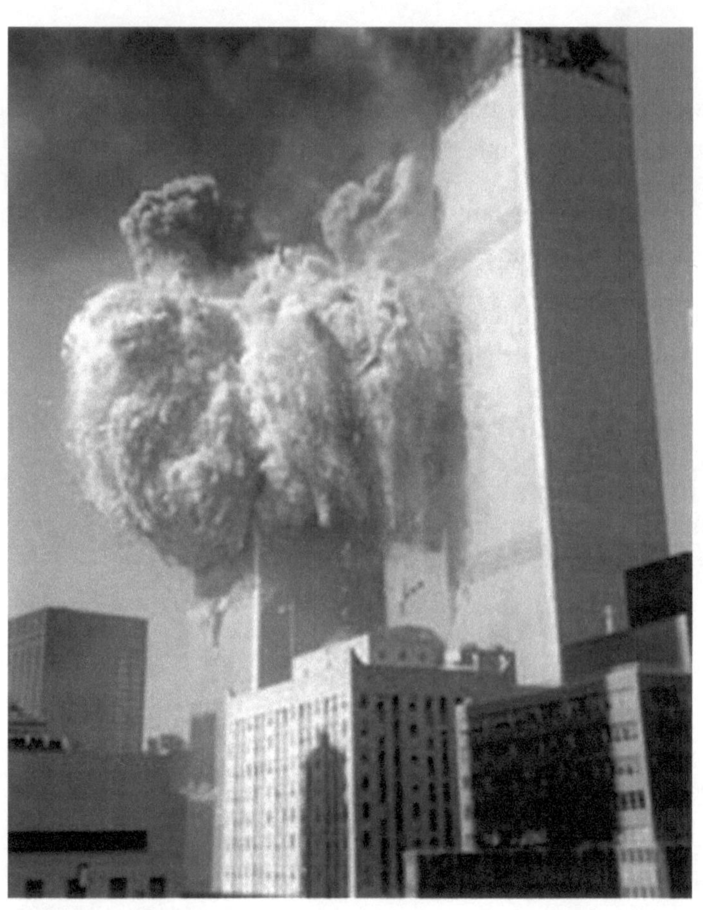

PREFACE

FOR A YEAR now, the poets, politicians, and pundits have tried to put the events of September 11, 2001 into some kind of historical perspective. Most of them have spoken from a narrow national and political perspective, while a minority have tried to deduce some spiritual implications of these world-shaking events. This book is among the latter.

I have taken the position that the events of September 11 forever changed the human concept of the divine. The Muslim terrorists thought that they were sacrificing themselves for God, but instead of exalting the Name of Allah, they destroyed forever the idea of a God who would demand suicide from His worshippers. Not only that, but they proved for all time that a God who sanctions the killing of thousands of innocents is a travesty that can only be invented by very sick minds.

At the same time, the vengeful and aggressive response of the religious West to the Muslim attacks was equally destructive of their idea of God as a compassionate and loving Father.

In the course of this book, I will try to show how what really died was the theistic concept of God. By theistic concept, I mean the idea of God as a separate deity, a separate Supreme Being, distinct from the Universe. The God of theism is somewhat akin to the God of Deism who was the favorite of our Masonic Founding Fathers. But the God of Deism is an aloof God, the Divine Architect, who planned and created the universe, then remains at a very safe distance, allowing the laws of nature which He created to run their course. The God of Theism, as taught by the three Monotheistic faiths is not aloof at all, but intervenes in history, and chooses certain people as His favorites, depending on which faith is writing its Sacred Books at the time.

In his now famous, or infamous, book, "Why Christianity Has To Change Or Die", Bishop Spong of the Episcopal Church points out in no uncertain terms that the God of Theism is dead. Who or what has taken God's place? Spong talks about "The Ground of Being", or "Ultimate Concern". For now, I will say that the God of Theism is a violation of the First Commandment against Idolatry. To make of God a"Supreme Being", All-knowing, All- powerful, is just as bad as making God into a Golden Calf.

The three monotheistic religions have made their God a tribal God who chose them, when in fact, they chose God and allocated Him to themselves.

When I say that God is not a separate being apart from the Universe, but rather that God IS all being, or rather the Ground of All Being, I am immediately accused of being a Pantheist, which is an outmoded way of thinking about God as being identical, or synonymous with the universe. But, they say, if everything is God and God is everything, Who is Who ? My response is that this idea of Pantheism is just as dead as the idea of Theism, for it is predicated on the idea of a theistic God who is a separate supreme being. Obviously a theistic God cannot be everything and everyone, and vice –versa, everything and everyone cannot be a theistic God. Who then, or what then, is God? Read on.

INTRODUCTION
HOW I BECAME GOD'S THERAPIST

WE ALL REMEMBER where we were on September 11, 2001 as we watched the Twin Towers of the World Trade Center disintegrate. I was having my breakfast in Salinas, California. My bags were packed, and I was about to leave for the Monterey Airport to fly back to New York. The day before, I had visited the incredible state of the art Museum dedicated to Salinas' most favored son, John Steinbeck. I had also watched most of Bill Moyers' tapes on James Campbell and the Power of Myth.

As I watched this once in a millennium event of the collapse of the two tallest skyscrapers in the world, I knew that I would never be the same again. I knew instinctively that the world had changed forever. Above all, I knew that all of mankind's most cherished images of God had gone down with the Twin Towers.

Needless to say, I was unable to fly home, and eventually ended up driving back : a thirty eight hour almost non-stop trip that turned out to be a pilgrimage, not only to the tomb of some 3,000 diverse Metropolitan New York citizens, but to the grave of the God of Theism at Ground Zero.

You see, I consider all events in the universe in relationship to what they say about God: whether they alter a previous perception of God, or perhaps destroy humankind's very concept of God. A good example of this, though in reverse, would be the fall of Communism in the Soviet Union. The demise of the Communist State was a death blow to Marx and Lenin's concept of God, or rather absence of God. The Communists said that religion was the opium of the people, because it allowed the masses to live for centuries under oppression while they looked forward to a reward after death. Dialectical materialism, on the other hand, set up a state based on atheism. Without a God to enforce the communal sharing of the earth, and without heaven or hell to straighten out the greed of humans in an after life, the Communists had to create a police state here on earth to force people to share the resources of the world. Now, after the collapse of Communism, their concept of godless materialism seems also to have died.

This book is the story of the development of my idea of God. Ever since I was old enough to entertain the concept of a Supreme Being, I have been fascinated with God's identity. You might say I have put more effort into finding out who God is than who I am. This is not merely an intellectual curiosity. It is emotional, spiritual, and even physical. You might say that my whole being has always been consumed with the search for God. In a sense, the search for God, for God's identity, became as it were MY identity. I became a God Searcher. Since I was born into the Roman Catholic tradition, it was only a matter of course that I entered the seminary at the age of thirteen, and after fourteen years of prayer and study, entered into the ministry to tell others about the God I knew. Then came one of those world-shaking events that inevitably altered my concept of God. The event was called Vatican Council II, in which all the Cardinals and Bishops of the world, together with representatives of all the Christian churches, met for four years, and called for 'updating' Christianity to fit the needs of the modern world. This truly cataclysmic council called for sweeping changes that more than doubled the changes of the Protestant Reformation in the 1500's. But somehow, the final drafts of the documents left out the most important changes that needed to be made, and the ones that remained were gradually stifled by the conservatives in the Vatican who had been opposed to any change from the beginning. I soon began to feel that I was operating with a concept of God that was very different from the "official" Church. The Church was teaching a God who was pre-packaged, and a finished product. The orthodox fundamentalists had taken over, and had declared that the so-called "deposit of faith" was closed with the death of the last

Apostle. They knew everything they needed to know about God this side of eternity, and they had been directly commissioned by God to impose their "magisterium" or " teaching authority" on the rest of the world. These were the same types who had told Galileo to shut up when he said the earth revolved around the sun instead of vice-versa, as the Bible says. Essentially, I felt that the Church had rejected the Einsteinian revolution of relativity, and had gone back to the absolutism of Vatican I, which took place in 1870.

But in the 1970's, I found myself going through a mid-life crisis, all because of my changing concept of God. I studied for a Master's degree in Psychiatric Social Work, and for my Master's thesis, I wrote a book on "The Mid-life Crisis As A Crisis of Meaning." In that study I showed that a change in our concept of God can lead to a nervous breakdown or worse for anyone who had depended on God to give meaning to life. I found a temporary solution to my dilemma in a theologian named "Paul Tillich" who said that his concept of God had changed into "The Ground of Being", or "Ultimate Concern." He wrote a book called, "The Courage To Be", in which he said that with the death of the old concept of God as a personal Father to each of us, we have to choose life as we find it, for better or worse. The only choice we have is to live or kill ourselves. He calls this the "Courage To Be", and what it amounts to is choosing to live a life with no meaning, for no reason, and that, in itself, imparts meaning to our existence. In other words, it is a most meaningful thing to live a human life for its own sake. Today I would say that life is a value in itself, and unless we create that value ourselves, by choosing life, we have no meaning. I would also say that our own mysterious participation in divinity shines through when we see the value in all of human life.

For twenty five years now, as a psychotherapist, I have been telling patients to "get a life", to choose life, in the sense that Tillich explains it. But for me, in the recession of the seventies, this 'leap of faith' in one's own human value without faith in God was much more difficult than all the previous leaps of faith that I had made with faith in God. Here I was, a defrocked priest, with no God and with no job. Here I was in Times Square, New York, without a God, without a woman, and without a golf swing. I had jokingly told my friends for years that the greatest mysteries in life were the Holy Trinity, woman, and the golf swing. I eventually took lessons to learn the golf swing, married a woman to study at first hand the mystery of the Feminine, and launched myself on a lifelong search for the God I sorely missed. There is no pain like the loneliness of missing God for one who has spent 50 years on a first name basis with God.

My first task was to answer the question: "Can God be known by human beings?" If God, by definition, is the infinite, limitless Being, can God be known by a finite, limited mind? Of course not. We are talking about knowing God as God is in Himself. As such, God cannot be known by the limited human mind. All we can know is our idea of God. I am aware that St. Paul says, "Now we see as in a glass, darkly, but then we shall know (God) even as we are known (by God.)" St. Paul, of course, is talking about what happens after death, another thing unknowable right now to limited human minds. So what we are talking about throughout this book is God as He is known by humans, that is, our human, limited idea of an unlimited God.

My second task was to understand the difference between myth and logos. Karen Armstrong, a former nun from England, wrote two books on the subject of God: "A History of God", and "The Battle For God". The first was the history of mankind's search for God, basically over the past three thousand years, especially in the three monotheistic religions. God for the Jews, Christians, and Muslims was basically the Supreme Being, a Pure Spirit, all-seeing, all-knowing, all- powerful, as opposed to the almost human gods of the Egyptian, Hindu, Greek, and Roman mythology. Traditionally, the three monotheistic faiths took their God literally, that is, as objectively real, or "logos", which means, in Greek, a logical reality, as opposed to the mythological gods who only existed as fantasies or far-flung metaphors for the hidden powers of the universe. Actually, the pagan gods were projections of mankind, made in our own image and likeness, "anthropomorphized" as the Greek philosophers would call them, or "with human form" in the Greek. What the monotheists did not understand was that their "Omnipotent Spirit" was not an objective reality either. Their idea of a spiritual omnipotent being was also myth and metaphor because that is the only way that human beings can talk about God.

How did the three Monotheistic religions get away with objectifying God as a special being, separate from the rest of the universe? They simply invented a gift of God called faith, which God only gave to certain people. With this gift of faith, they were able to know God as a separate being, that is, a supernatural being, above nature. Thus, these divine religions or faiths have survived through scientific breakthroughs, reformations, renaissances, modernizations, and technological revolutions. Every time the secular scholars try to tell them that there is no provable scientific reality out there, at least no separate Supreme Being, the believers just reiterate that it's a matter of faith not science.

Another way of talking about the difference between myth and logos is to use the phrase 'symbol versus literalism.' An Australian theologian named Michael Morwood has written two books explaining the difference between symbol and literalism in religion. In *Tomorrow's Catholic: Understanding God and Jesus in the New Millennium* and *Is Jesus God? Finding* Our *Faith,* Morwood explains in great detail how we can no longer hold on to the traditional, literal teachings of the church and of religion, because the incredible knowledge explosion of the cyber age has proven that these teachings are only symbols and metaphors, not to be taken literally, and we need a whole new way of thinking about God and Jesus.

Now that we have come to the Third Millennium, science seems to be overcoming the traditional faiths, and this is where Armstrong's second book, "The Battle For God" comes in. She talks about what happens when the fundamentalists of all faiths refuse to accept the fact that their most cherished ideas of God are "only myths", or "only metaphors", as opposed to objective reality. Of course, all the orthodox fundamentalists of all faiths believe that their God is objectively real and they know him by faith, a special grace which God has given to them alone. Of course, they become quite incensed when so-called "liberals" and "relativists" tell them that no matter how much grace God gives them, they are still human and humans can only know unconscious and hidden reality by metaphor or myth. Humans can only say, "God is LIKE this"(metaphor), or "It's as if God WERE this" (myth). All the while, as humans, we are painfully aware that God is more UNLIKE our myths and metaphors, than He is like them !

Now, as Karen Armstrong says, when the fundamentalists hear this, they go berserk, and immediately adopt the siege mentality, in fear of annihilation. When we destroy their image of God, we are threatening their whole way of life, not only - but their way of death, and life after death- in short, the whole meaning of their existence. In other words, the fundamentalists of the world, especially the Muslim fundamentalists who never had a reformation like the Jews and Christians, are now facing the fear of annihilation. They are going through a crisis of meaning much like the one that led me out of the Catholic Priesthood. I can now understand somewhat their fear of annihilation, though it can never justify the vicious annihilation of innocents that they are guilty of. I am painfully aware that if this book is a success, they will probably put out a fatwah against me as an enemy of Allah. But you can imagine how they will feel when they find out that heaven is a metaphor, and the virgins in paradise are a myth, all 75 of them.

But if they wish, perhaps they can learn from my experience. I have struggled over the past twenty five years to come up with an accommodation to the Death of God which I suffered through in the seventies. I have learned to pick and choose the myths of God that spoke to my personal unconscious, which, of course, is somehow connected to the Collective Unconscious. I also learned to adapt the individual myths that no longer spoke to me so that I could then relate to them personally. For instance, I no longer see God as Our Father in heaven, but more like Our Mother on earth. I no longer see Jesus as God, but as the Compassion of God, knowing that these too, are still myths, or symbols but myths and symbols that I can participate in personally. After all, the very idea of myth comes from the Greek mystery religions, where the initiates participate through rituals in the life of the gods. That is why the metaphor of the Eucharist, the Thanksgiving over Bread and Wine, allowing us to participate in the mystery of our Oneness, no matter what we believe about God, has survived for so long. I know I need a worshiping community which honors any myths that I can relate to or adapt to, as I continue my search for God.

The " therapy sessions for God" which I am about to share are a natural continuation in my search, since I am both a God Searcher and a Psychotherapist. They were not planned, they were not even fantasized in advance. They just happened, had a life span of their own, as any of a hundred therapies that I have done with patients over the past twenty five years. This round of therapy was much faster than most. After all the Patient was smarter than all the others.

But, in reality, as opposed to myth, the Patient is not really God as God is in Herself, but rather my idea of God as it developed over the past 72 years. Another way of saying it is: I have internalized God, made a separate person out of Her in my mind, just as I have internalized my parents, my siblings, my wife, and all the significant persons in my life..

Remember, these internalizations are all metaphors and myths. The only objective reality is myself, and you, and the universe, and all the people who love us. Maybe that's the closest we'll ever get to knowing WHO GOD IS.

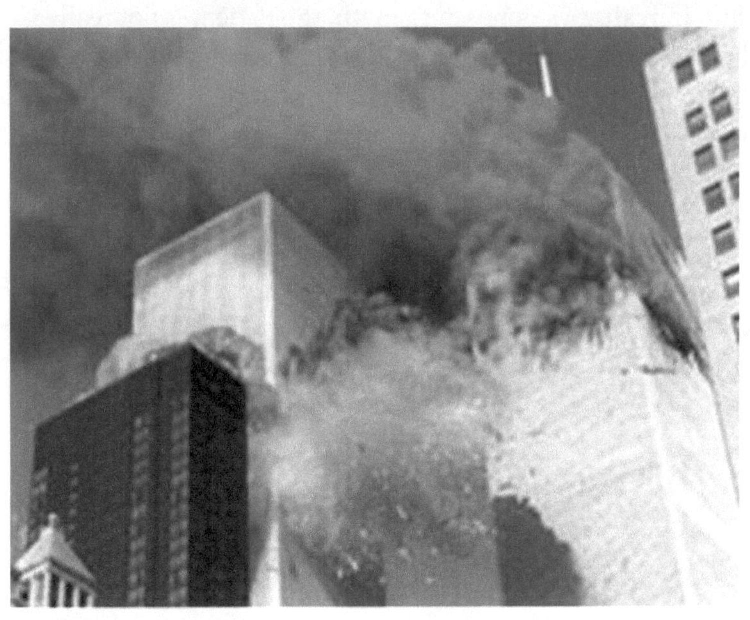

DOING THERAPY FOR GOD

(This was written the second Sunday after the Bombings.)

GOD CAME TO me this morning and asked for a therapy session. I told her,"Why are you coming to me ? This afternoon at 2:30 there will be a huge religious service at Yankee Stadium. The Cardinal Archbishop Of NY will be there, all the other Bishops from the metropolitan area will be there. All the Protestant and Orthodox leaders will be there. The Jewish rabbis : the Othodox, Conservative, Reformed, even the Hassidim will be there. The Imams from all the Muslim Mosques, even from Malcom (X) Shabazz will be there. The Hindus, the Sikh's, the Shintos, the Buddhists, even the Pagan Druids will be there, even the Chinese who believe that you are their grandmother will be there. Go there and you'll feel better."

It was then that God broke out into uncontrollable weeping. She shook so bad, I thought she was having a nervous breakdown. Then she began, "Sure they'll all be there, and they will be everywhere in the world : the believers in me. The Muslims, who call themselves Islam: People of God ; the Jews, who call themselves People of God ; The Christians who call themselves People of God ; all the people of the earth who acknowledge me as Earth Mother, Creator, Higher Power, Great Spirit, Whatever, Whatever. They all regard themselves as my children. But they have spent all of history hating each other, hurting each other, killing each other. It's bad enough that they do this to others, but why do they have to do it in My Name?"

God then broke into even deeper sobs, and I really was afraid she was going to lose it. So I tried to distract her with this little ditty to the tune of "America the Beautiful". I told her that even though I was a Christian, I could still sing this song for my Muslim brothers and sisters.

(Salaam means Peace.)

"Islam The Beautiful" to the tune of "America The Beautiful"
"Salaam, Islam, Salaam Islaam Allah be good to you.
To Arabs all, and Farsi, too, All Muslims black and brown.
Allah look down, Bless all of you, And give you Peace at home.
Salaam Islam, Salaam Islam Allah be good to you."

At first God thought I might be losing it myself with the likes of this little ditty, then She calmed down a little bit, and seemed to be okay for the moment. But what do I tell her when she comes back for her next session?

P.S. I wrote this session this morning (Sunday, the 23rd) but didn't have time to finish it. In the meantime, Peggy and I spent about four hours watching the stirring ceremonies at Yankee Stadium, commemorating all the deceased, and grieving with their families. I am sure God got a lot of encouragement from the program. I am sure that She is going to be all right. But am I going to be all right ? It ain't easy being God's therapist, especially when she is having a nervous breakdown.

God's Second Therapy Session

God had calmed down a great deal from her nervous breakdown of Sept. 11. But now She was deep into a clinical depression. "When my Muslim boys hit the first tower, I wept. When they slammed into the second tower, I began to sob uncontrollably. When one tower began to go down, I felt myself sinking into the earth. When the second tower collapsed, I shuddered and died. People all over the world were whispering in some 138 languages, 'God just died.' In every dialect of every tongue on earth they gasped, 'This is the Grave of God !' Even Islamist fundamentalists shuddered to think that Allah had had it this time. ' No more Allah, no more Akbar. No more Allah to be praised. This is what Satan had always wanted and now he has won.' But the Chinese and the Japanese- you can all thank me that I made a few billion of those brilliant almond-eyed beauties. They did not weep or wail for Me. They turned as usual to their ancestors and found peace in the living souls of those who went before them."

But then I consoled God with Her beautiful animals. I told Her how splendid the animals have been throughout this tragedy. "They didn't question You, " I said. " They went about their business of living, accepting life as it is given to them, extremely grateful for every moment granted to them. They are your glory, God. They do You proud. But we humans, all we give You is grief. First we find You, then we lose You, then we adore You, then we kill You. Don't blame Yourself. I'll see you same time next week.

God looked only a little comforted, but not much. She left the session still in a deep depression.

GOD'S THIRD THERAPY SESSION.

I have heard that there are over two hundred thousand persons in Nassau County (here in Long Island) who are in need of bereavement counseling, not to mention the thousands of others, indeed, all of us, who need counseling for anxiety. So I may not have time to do any more Therapy with God, (Not that God is not suffering more than any of us from this unspeakable act of horror.)For her third session, God was still shaking uncontrollably, and I diagnosed her as suffering from Post-Traumatic Stress Syndrome. I had prepared for her session by re-reading the Diagnostic Manual on PTSS. " *Diminished responsiveness to the external world, referred to as 'psychic numbing', or 'emotional anesthesia'. The individual may complain of having markedly diminished interest or participation in previously enjoyed activities, of feeling detached or estranged from other people, or of having markedly reduced ability to feel emotions, especially those associated with intimacy, tenderness, and sexuality. The individual may have a sense of a foreshortened future, e.g. not expecting to have a career, marriage, children, or a normal life span. The individual has persistent symptoms of anxiety, which may include difficulty falling or staying asleep that may be due to recurrent nightmares during which the traumatic event is relived.*"

Come to think of it, the entire nation, and probably most of the rest of the world is suffering from Post-Traumatic Stress Syndrome. So how could God not be suffering her worst case ever of PTSS ? God didn't even want to speak. But finally She said, " I think I have lost interest in the world. " But I told her immediately, " the world hasn't lost interest in You ! People are flocking to churches, synagogues, temples, mosques, everywhere." But all God could say was, "There are no atheists in foxholes. The world has become one huge foxhole, and people everywhere feel they are under siege, and they only turn to me because they are in terror and have nowhere else to turn. But they don't really believe in me, they don't really love Me. As soon as the Dow Jones hits 11000 again, they'll forget all about me."

Then she went on, " Look what happened in the Deluge. I know it's only a myth, but as soon as Noah landed on dry land, he forgot all about God and got drunk."

"Look what happened after Pearl Harbor. They sang, 'Praise the Lord, and pass the ammunition, and we'll all be free.' Why, back in the time of Constantine, he led the Roman Legions with the Cross of Christ, ' In this sign you shall conquer.' Then along came Mohammed and his believers in Allah and by the sword converted most of Africa, Asia, and a large part of Europe to Islam. And now George W. is calling for another Crusade (even though he retracted it, we all know what he meant) to kill some more in MY Name. No wonder I need psychotherapy !"

But I said, "God, God, God, look at all the Love that has come out of this tragedy, Look at all the husbands and wives, mothers and fathers and children, who frantically called on their cell phones, and wept how much they loved each other. Since You are Love, you were there in the midst of them, and still you remain. Don't hold back that Love now, God, we need you more than ever. Don't try to protect your broken heart by not caring about us anymore. Your heart is broken precisely because you *ARE CARE*, and *ULTIMATE CONCERN*."

Did my little speech make God feel any better? Stay tuned.

GOD'S FOURTH THERAPY SESSION

I could tell that God was very angry when she showed up for her fourth therapy session. My patients are always angry after I take a vacation. Some are so angry that they don't show up. But I have to tell you, God showed up. "So how was Golf School?" she asked.

"Oh, I enjoyed it very much !" I said.

"Well, I don't see any improvement in your golf swing !" God quipped.

"Maybe not",I answered,"but now I feel a lot better about myself as a golfer, because now I know what I have been doing wrong."

"What's so good about that ?"

God was getting petulant, so I said,"That's why people come to therapy: to find out what they have been doing wrong. When they see themselves clearly as others see them, they may not change right away, and they may not stop doing all those self-defeating behaviors that make them feel so bad, but now they feel a lot better about themselves because they understand what and why about themselves."

Now She was really mad. " So what have I been doing to make myself feel so bad ?"

This is the opening that I was looking for." Why do you allow so many kooks in this world to think they are speaking for you?"

"Why do YOU ALWAYS THINK YOU ARE SPEAKING FOR ME ?"

"I wasn't talking about ME, I was talking about Osama BinLaden, Gerry Falwell, Pope John Paul II, and the rest of the Fundamentalists of every so called faith in YOU.!"

We were shouting real loud at each other. Man, did we have the old Freudian transference-countertransference thing going between God and me!

God said, " What's the difference between your conceit that you speak for me, and all the orthodox fundamentalists of the world's conceit that they speak for ME ? What's the difference between Rudy Giuliani's and George Bush's conceit that they speak for ME, and YOUR conviction that you speak for ME?"

Man, was she mad ! I tried to explain to her that she was simply transferring to me her anger towards all the right wing fundamentalists who are giving HER such a bad name. I said to HER, "At the beginning of this session I tried to tell you that therapy is all about recognizing your self-defeating behaviors. You have been defeating yourself by letting the Jews, the Muslims, the Christians, all the TRUE BELIEVERS of this world, think that they have a hot-line to God, that they are the only ones who know what YOU want. The reason why you have been so depressed since Sept. 11 is that you are so disappointed at all the so-called People of Faith who pretend to speak for you, and then go against your very nature as LOVE and go out and dominate, oppress, hate, and kill, all in your NAME ? This anger of yours is a good beginning. It shows that you are beginning to understand the mistake you have made. You know what you have been doing wrong. Your depression will go away when you accept that you have been simply giving in to your own nature as Love. Maybe you won't change, maybe the fundamentalists won't change, but you and they will at least know what they are doing wrong."

God looked puzzled. I don't think She got the message. Maybe I didn't either.

GOD'S FIFTH THERAPY SESSION

God came roaring into her fifth therapy session like she was on a mission. She could not wait to get started, in fact she started before I sat down.

"You know Carl Jung, the psychologist who first discovered the collective unconscious, was the son and the grandson of Swiss Reformed Ministers. When he was seven years old he had a vision while walking home from school one day. The vision shocked him so much that he did not have the courage to tell anybody about it until he was over 70 years old !"

"What was the vision about ?" I asked, just to assure Her that I was listening. "Carl Jung was passing by his father's church, and he heard a rumble like thunder out of heaven, and he looked up and a huge rear end was sticking out of the sky and pooping on his father's church! It took Jung over sixty years to reveal that vision because it was too scary for him to think that God was so mad at the church."

"How mad are you at the church?", I asked.

"I'm so mad at the church that I could scream ! But it's not the people in the church who really love Me that upset me so. It's mostly church *men* that I cannot stand. For the past three thousand years, at least, the men in the three monotheistic faiths have acted as if they owned me. It was men who wrote all the scriptures, and of course they all claimed to be directly inspired by Me ! Even you pretend to know exactly what I want. You and all the rest of those men! You don't know me! You have oppressed women for three thousand years. How could you be so callous and domineering to women and still pretend to know Me, the Earth Mother? Well you are all just spoiled Momma's Boys, and since I am the Great Momma, I take the blame for all of you. But no more! I've had it with all you rigid, pretentious, authoritarian know-it-all's."

The Feminist Movement had come full circle from Dana the Earth Goddess to the Immanent God of the Pantheists.

What could I say to Her?

"Would it help if we now prayed to you:

"Our Mother who art on earth,
"Your Name is very holy,
"Make us whole, and holy and healers like You
"Help all your children do your loving Will,
"Both in time and in eternity.
"Give us each day what we need. "Help us
forgive ourselves first "And then one another.
"Don't let us ever lose sight of You
"For that is the only evil"
"For yours is the praise,
the honor, and the glory.
"Forever, Amen."
Let's all hope it made God feel better.

God's Sixth Therapy Session

Before God's sixth Session, I was on the phone with Medicare. Some bureaucrat refused to pay for my therapy for God on the grounds that she was ineligible.

"But she's 13 Billion Years old !" I cried. "That may be so, but she only worked for 6 days, and you need forty quarters to qualify for Medicare."

(Not only a bureaucrat, but a Creationist and fundamentalist to boot.) "And besides," says the bureaucrat, "It would be against the separation of church and state for the government to pay for God's therapy."

"But this God doesn't belong to any church," I said, " In fact, She is an atheist, and doesn't even believe in the God of the Churches."

"Well, if She's that screwed up, she certainly needs treatment, but she's God, so She can pay for her own treatment !"

When God came in for her eighth session I told her about the Medicare Bureaucrat. She became inconsolable.

"I'm a failure as a Creator, " she wept. " How did I manage to create so many mean-spirited, rigid believers?"

"It's not Your fault" I said. "You created a beautiful universe, but you chose to make us free, and too many of us are afraid of freedom. We need too much love and compassion to be free. It's much easier to give up freedom in favor of law.

"I remember the great theologian, Bernard Haring, saying that there is an inverse proportion between love and law. The more love we have for each other, the less law we need, and vice-versa. But humans have so little faith that they need facts to believe in. They have so little trust in each other that they have to make rules to protect themselves. They have so little love that they need thousands of laws, and millions of regulations to keep us from devouring each other. There goes the freedom with which you created us. We are all living in a prison."

I am afraid that my political posturing and futile philosophy was all lost on God.

She sighed, " Why can't they just give joy to their Mother's heart and love one another as Abraham, Moses, Jesus, Mohammed, Confucius, Buddha, Joseph Smith, and all the other prophets told them to do ?"

GOD'S SEVENTH THERAPY SESSION

Before God's Seventh Therapy Session, I took some time to ponder what was happening in the therapy. In every successful course of treatment there is analysis of the counter-transference and transference. Since God's transference to me is unknowable, the whole burden of this treatment will depend on the success of my analysis of my own counter- transference. Usually, I get help from a supervisory analyst for this purpose, but in this case, most supervisory analysts won't believe I really have a patient. So I am unfortunately on my own.

Counter-transference means that the therapist projects his (her) unconscious feelings, needs, desires onto the patient. In this case was I unconsciously wishing for a God who would be loving and compassionate, forgiving and merciful, provident, and yes, maternal? Freud had said that God was a sublimation, that we unconsciously longed for a Father Figure, and the God of the scriptures was just that and no more, a projection. Is it possible that my God is a projection of an aging man who is reverting to childhood and unconsciously looking for a Mother to take care of him in his second childhood?

Be that as it may, when God came in for her ninth session, I asked her what I ask all of my patients around this time.

"Are you getting out of treatment what you came for?"

"Not really," She answered.

"Well, what did You come for ?", I asked.

"I came to get some sense out of the tragedy of Sept. 11, and out of all the madness that followed it."

"What do You mean by that ?", I asked in order to get Her deeper into Her depression

"I still find no reason for the senseless killing of innocents," She answered.

I felt like Job in the Hebrew Bible, except that God was taking Job's role, and sticking me with God's, which is the hard part.

"There is no reason, there is no sense to it all, " I answered. "How can I make sense of it for You? You're God after all ! The only answer faith gets anymore is doubt, and the only answer to hope is despair.

"I was talking with a fireman last Sunday, who is a recovering alcoholic. For the past two years his job has been to counsel his fellow firemen, and conduct Alcoholics Anonymous groups in the Fire Department. He has been to all 270 Firehouses twice during the past two months, and they have all given up faith in God. Those who had been in recovery before Sept. 11 have all gone back to drinking. Forget about 'Let go, let God, Go God' the first three steps of AA. There is no Higher Power for them any more. How can the Higher Power save them if it let the Twin Towers fall? As far as they are concerned, God is dead!"

God was appalled. " I don't care if they don't believe in ME anymore. I still believe in THEM. But the ones who kill in MY NAME, kill themselves in MY NAME, making HOLY WAR ? What kind of Satan inspired them to HOLY WAR ? I am feeling like I did before the Deluge. I am sorry I made these people."

"Wait a minute, Earth Mother, maybe this Holy War is the final battle between the Father God and the Mother God, between the God of Justice and Vengeance, Commandments and Punishment, and the God of Love and Compassion? Does that mean anything to You?"

"Yes," God finally said, after a lengthy pause, "It means that My therapist has finally flipped his lid."

Well- that was the best that I could do. At least it made God smile.

GOD'S EIGHTH THERAPY SESSION

Before God's eighth therapy session, I was on the phone with managed care to see how many sessions the insurance company would give me for God. They said there was only a medical necessity for ten sessions. I was infuriated.

"You mean this patient has had this problem for 13 Billion years, and you expect me to straighten her out in ten sessions?"

They answered that I could write a letter of appeal asking for ten more sessions if I could prove medical necessity. It was a recorded message, and said press number 8 for address for letter of appeal. I hung up in disgust, and decided to charge Medicare for these sessions, even though Medicare only gives a pittance to Social Workers that is not even enough to pay for office rent.

When God came in for her session, I knew right away that I had made her wait too long since the last session. She was obviously upset, annoyed, and irritated, her affect flat, and her mood depressed.

"I have decided to become an atheist," she announced.

Thank God I held back and did not remark that this was a contradiction in terms: God cannot stop believing in God. She went right on, "Not that I don't believe in Myself anymore, but I have become an atheist because we atheists don't believe in religion. Atheists don't have a problem with God because as far as they are concerned He doesn't exist. But atheists have a big problem with *religion*, especially organized religion. Most of the problems I have had all through history are with them. They are an embarrassment and a disgrace to Me. Especially the fundamentalist branches of Judaism, Christianity, and Islam. They are all so pretentious that they are sure that they know what I want, even though they constantly contradict and kill one another. The only thing they agree on is that women must be kept 'in their place', and they are totally blind to the fact that the male principle of law is opposed to the female principle of love. No wonder you have diagnosed Me as schizophrenic."

I tried to inject a little humor into this very serious session.

"I'll grant you that the organized religions are pretty bad, but the disorganized religions are even worse. Look at the Holy Warriors of Allah, the Islamic Jihad, the Hezbollah. They are right up there with the organized religions giving you a bad name.

She got the joke. "You can thank me that the Chinese worship their grandmothers. That gets Me off the hook every time."

It's always good to let your patients ventilate. They invariably feel better until next session.

GOD'S NINTH THERAPY SESSION

God was even more depressed when She came in for her Ninth Session..

"I feel very, very guilty for becoming an atheist and giving up on God for good"

"You have *not* become an atheist, or given up on Yourself."

"What does *that* mean?"

"I am trying to say that atheism does not apply to You!"

"What?"

"Atheism is based on *theism*. Now theism is the belief that there is one monotheistic God who is The Supreme Being, separate from all visible reality, totally transcending the created universe.

"Atheism is the refusal to believe in *that* kind of God. For 3000 years now, we have allowed the three monotheistic religions: Judaism, Christianity, and Islam, to define God for us as this separate Supreme Being and thus they have defined atheists as anyone who refuses to believe in *their* idea of God.

"The Greeks and the Romans did the same thing: they called Jews and Christians *atheists*, not because they did not believe in God, but because they did not believe in the Greek or Roman idea of God!"

"Why am I having so much trouble understanding what all these various religions think I am?"

"Because the God of the Bible and of the Q'uran is a very mean-spirited God who is both immoral and unbelievable."

"Man, are you looking for an anathema or a fatwah against you?"

"Read your own Bible and Q'uran which the orthodox and fundamentalists claim was dictated directly by You!", I answered.

"The Bible is about a tribal God who gets so mad he destroys all living things in a flood, except for Noah's family and the pairs of animals birds, and insects on the ark."

"Except, of course, the poor, dear, little unicorns, which were too playful to come on board,!" God sighs.

"What kind of God would be so mean as to destroy his own beautiful creatures he just took several billion years to make?

"Then the twelve tribes of Israel get out of Egypt, led by this same mean- spirited God who heartlessly sends blood, locusts, and frogs, and ends up slaughtering the first-born son of every Egyptian family in the country! Then, to make sure the poor punished Egyptians die anyway, this God of Israel 'hardens Pharaoh's heart,' so he goes after Moses and the twelve tribes and gets drowned by God in the Red Sea."

"Who wants to believe in a God like that?" she said.

"Then the Christian part of the Bible is even worse: God kills his own son because he is so offended by our sins that only a divine person, shedding his divine blood can save us?

"What kind of perverted God is that? (Jack Miles, in his book, *Christ: a Crisis in the Life of God*, calls this a suicidal God.)

"Then, I hardly have to mention Islam and it's Allah, who from the beginning, commanded His followers to convert, or kill, right up to today, with all the suicide bombers and terrorists trying to kill 'infidels', which means people who don't believe the exact same things about Allah that they believe!"

"But who, literally, in hell would want to believe in a God like that?"

"No wonder we are all becoming Atheists with a God like that threatening the bejeebers out of us!"

"Then again, the God of the Bible and Q'uran is totally unbelievable in this, the age of evolution, relativity, and cosmic consciousness. Why John Shelby Spong quotes his friend, Carl Sagan, as laughing at the idea of Christ and Mohammed ascending into heaven.Why just our galaxy, alone, is 100,000 light years across, so in2000 years, Christ and his Arab friend, Mohammed, would only be 2% of the way out of our galaxy and then still have several more 'billions and billions, and billions' of galaxies to go through to get out of the universe into heaven: wherever in hell *that is!*"

God looked at me with a quizzical look as if to say: "This time my little Sicilian therapist has gone too far!"

GOD'S TENTH THERAPY SESSION

When God came for Her Tenth Session, I knew immediately that I had gone too far in my last session.

"I have decided to sue you for malpractice," She said. "I am suing you for 100 million dollars for breach of confidentiality. It has come to my attention that you have been sending these sessions out on the internet to your relatives and friends, and revealing my identity."

I almost thought that She was turning into the mean-spirited God of the Bible and Q'uran.

"Besides," she said, "Most of that stuff you threw at Me was stolen from John Shelby Spong and Michael Morwood. (Please see Bibliography to this book.) So I can get you for plagiarism if for nothing else!"

"Hold it, Heavenly Mother," I said, " I did not break confidentiality by revealing Your identity. First of all, I don't *know* who you are. Secondly, I explicitly stated that God as She is in Herself is unknowable by finite human minds. So what identity was I giving away? And surely, you are not going to sue me for attacking that mean-spirited, killer God of the Bible and Q'uran?"

"Tell it to the judge," She said. "You will be hearing from my lawyer, shortly!"

I resisted the temptation to say, 'Who is your lawyer, Saint Michael the Archangel or Rudy Giuliani ?'

Instead, I pleaded, "Wait a minute. I only have coverage for one million dollars. I'm just a Social Worker, for God's sake."

It always seems to happen to me when I am doing a good therapy. I run the gamut from positive transference on the part of the patient towards me to negative transference; to projection, denial, to quitting, and sometimes to suing. It's the only way I have of knowing that I'm doing my therapy right.

But it's a lot like Murphy's Law, too: if anything *can go wrong, it will go wrong.* In this case, it could be the Peter Principle, too, because treating God is way beyond my level of competence.

I think my Patient was giving me an unconscious signal to retreat.

"Can't we just talk?," I asked. "About what?"

"How did I hurt You by sharing these therapy sessions as E-mails?"

"People are not ready to hear that there's something wrong with God. It scares them!"

Here I was, making my usual mistake in doing therapy. I have this terrible tendency to make my patients stronger than they actually are. I keep forgetting that everybody who comes to therapy comes because they are in trouble. I have confessed this mistake all my life in supervision. First, because I am such an optimist, I tend to make patients much healthier than they actually are, completely forgetting why they came to me in the first place. Secondly, I am afraid to admit that they are actually very disturbed, because then I will not know how to treat them. But mostly, I am very lazy, and if I admit that my patients are severely disturbed, it's going to be a long, drawn-out labor for me. I hate work. When it is finally done, I look back at it with satisfaction and fulfillment, but like any tough job I've ever had to do in my life, when it's only beginning, I tend to deny the patient is as bad as she seems to be.

So I courageously decided to go against my tendency to deny how disturbed this patient was, especially since this One had the uncanny ability to read my mind.

"Well, God, I am sure that you just heard what I was thinking! You are telling me that 'people' aren't ready to hear there's something wrong with God!. I think You aren't ready to hear there's something wrong with You! So how can I help You?"

God looked at me with a wink of that Deistic Eye over a pyramid on the back of the One Dollar bill and said, "After these last two sessions, who needs therapy more: the Patient or the therapist?"

And she silently slipped away

GOD'S ELEVENTH THERAPY SESSION

I am happy to inform you that God was feeling a lot better when She came in for her eleventh session. Needless to say, I did not hear from her lawyer, but God had undergone some kind of inner transformation.

"I feel as if I have recovered from schizophrenia," She said with a great sigh of relief "Since mankind first sensed My presence in the universe, I have been made shizophrenic by them. I have been split between male and female, heavenly father and earth mother, God of Good/ God of Evil, God of the Prophets, God of the Philosophers. Now I no longer feel schizoid. I feel I am One. I feel I am back in the age of Gaia, The Earth Mother, when God and earth were one, when all creation was a Virgin Birth."

"That's beautiful," I said, " Karen Armstrong has written a book about you called, 'The Battle For God', which is about the rise of fundamentalism in the world's great religions. The terrorists were fundamentalists who thought they were fighting to hold on to a God that the humanist-secularists,(read America and the West) were trying to destroy. But the terrorists were sadly mistaken. The real battle is between the idea of a transcendent God and the idea of an immanent God. Isn't that why the Hindus and the Muslims hate each other so profoundly? The Hindus with their immanent earthy God, and the Muslims with their totally spiritual transcendent God? Isn't that why India split fifty years ago ? Their two ideas of God were incompatible!"

God said, "You may be right. Maybe this 'First World War' of the Twenty First Century' is about God. Many are saying this is really a religious war."

I foolishly pretended to explain it all to God.

"For the past two thousand years, the three monotheistic religions of the earth have made you into a transcendent God, a Sacred Other, a Being apart from the visible universe. And thus they were able to push you away from their real lives. They were really practicing idolatry, making You into the Almighty Helper in Heaven who would take care of them, and reward the good and punish the evil. And of course each religion defined the other religion as the bad guys who were going to be punished by the scary idol in the sky for not believing in the exact same way that they did. Now that everyone feels threatened with annihilation, hopefully they will turn to the God inside themselves: the immanent God, "In whom we live and move, and have our being", according to St. Paul. Let's hope they will stop and reflect, withdraw within themselves into their own depths where they come forth from the earth mother. Then they will realize that they cannot be annihilated because they already are part of the earth. Maybe they will understand that the heavenly God was blown up on Sept. 11, and the only God left is the earthly God in the ashes, alive and well, and She really loves New York! Is there an earthier place on earth than New York?"

God gave me that annoyed look that patients always give me when I talk more about my own ideas than about them. So I apologized to Her and said that this was more a therapy session for me than for Her, but all she said was, I needed it more than She did.

GOD'S TWELFTH THERAPY SESSION

In preparation for God's twelfth therapy session, I consulted a psychologist for supervision. I wanted to make sure that I was not projecting all my unconscious feelings and needs onto my Patient. Together we agreed that my Patient was not suffering from schizophrenia nor was She even schizoid. She was still suffering from Post-Traumatic Stress Syndrome. We ruled out Gender Identity Disorder, because She was handling all the negative masculine projections that the monotheistic religions had foisted on Her. But her real problem was She was going through an Identity Crisis. According to Eric Erickson, we all go through an identity crisis between the ages of 13 and 21.Its onset usually signals the beginning of adolescence (around puberty time), and its resolution signals the beginning of young adulthood. Now, of course, my Patient is thirteen, but we're talking 13 Billion here. Will God's identity crisis go on for another 7 Billion years, give or take a Billion or two? Does that mean, with the present life expectancy of around 85, that we can presume that the Universe is going to last for 85 Billion years? Something for Stephen Hawking to ponder, and perhaps write a book about.

My task now was to help my patient figure out who She was, because no one can solve their identity crisis alone. When God was slightly younger, She answered Moses' query, "Who are you?" with the simple Hebrew, "Yah-weh", which translates, "I am Who I am", or simply, "I'm Me". Actually, it was a very Jewish answer: Why do you ask who I am, I'm Me ! I'm the One you're talking to, dummy." Some philosophers among the believers have since tried to interpret this in a very metaphysical way and say, "I am Who am" means, "I am Being Itself", or "Pure Being", but obviously the Hebrew writer had no intention of revealing God's identity, because he had no idea what God was or identity was.

Later on, in the Christian scriptures, Jesus is going through his own identity crisis, and asks everyone, "Who do men say that I am?"

The writer at that time was obviously using this as a literary device to express his opinion of who Jesus was.

"You are the Christ (The Anointed One), the Son of the Living God."

Even though we now know that this was only meant metaphorically, it did express the author's feelings about Jesus. Now, as I analyze God, are these therapy sessions just a literary device on my part to express my opinion of who God is? Very good preparation for God's Thirteenth Therapy Session.

God's Thirteenth Therapy Session

When God came in for Her thirteenth session, I decided to attack Her Identity Problem head on. I asked Her, "What do You think is wrong with You?"

I know that this is a stupid question, and I would never use it with a human patient, but after all She is God, so I felt that She could take it.

"If I knew what was wrong with Me, I wouldn't need therapy would I ?" She answered smartly. "You're the therapist, what do YOU think is wrong with Me?"

"You are having an identity crisis" I answered, "But don't worry, it's very age appropriate. We all reach a point in life where we need to know who we are, as opposed to anyone else."

"What's wrong with the answer I gave Moses ?", she retorted, "I'm Me." She actually sounded like a teenage girl when She said it.

"I'm sorry, God, but You know that wasn't an answer. Who are You, as opposed to everyone else and everything else in the universe, as opposed to the Universe itself ?"

"It's easier to say who I am NOT. I am not "A Being", I am not "A God", I am not "A Divine Person", definitely not " A Trinity of Divine Persons." Talk about a schizoid personality! If being split in two is bad, how would you like to be split in Three? Is that a multiple personality syndrome or what: Trinophrenia?

"I am definitely not Allah. Not the Christian God of the Crusaders and George Bush! 'Onward Christian soldiers' indeed! Anybody who makes God into a separate Being apart from the Universe is an idolater."

I immediately broke in, "But that means that all of the believers in the monotheistic religions are idolaters. That means that all Muslims are infidels, all Jews are breaking the First Commandment, all Christians are infidels and idolaters, especially the ones who believe that Christ is God"

"No, not ALL of them," She said, " only the fundamentalists, only the ones who take their scriptures as literal logos rather than myth."

"But almost all Jews, Muslims, and Christians believe God is a Divine Person",I said.

"Then they are fundamentalists, infidels, and idolaters, "God answered. "They need to re-read their scriptures. What I was inspiring their Scripture Writers to say was myth, metaphor, a manner of speaking that could not fully express unconscious being. You, my therapist, are an infidel and idolater if you really think I am a Divine Person talking to you right now as you write.

I assured Her that I did NOT think She was a Divine Person, but was the Ground of Being, or Ultimate Concern, somehow accessing my unconscious, and I loved her very much Whoever or Whatever She was. God was relieved to hear that I at least got that one right. But She still hadn't solved Her Identity Problem.

"What else are you NOT ?" I asked.

"I am not Allah, the God of Holy War. There is no such thing as a Holy War. I am not the Allah who smiles on suicidal fanatics who slaughter my children unmercifully, viciously, and satanically. I am not George W. Bush's God of 'Infinite Justice' who slaughters more innocents, who really is the God of Vengeance, and a throwback to the Nazi God of 'Might makes Right', in disguise."

At least God knows who She ISN'T. I can't wait for Her to tell us Who She IS.

God's Fourteenth Therapy Session

I pondered how to handle my Divine Adolescent in Her fourteenth. therapy session, and consulted a specialist in the psychology of adolescence. He pointed out immediately that adolescence is characterized by dizzying and disorienting change, especially rapid-fire change that turns one's self-image topsy-turvy. Just as early toddlerhood brought the child full circle from omnipotence to incompetence, adolescence brought the latent child from dependency and innocence to rebellion. Sure sounded like my patient : the rebellion part, that is When She came in for Her session, I asked her if she was ready to identify Herself. "No, I'm not," She said, " I'm not finished telling you who I am not."

"Let's hear it, "I answered.

"I am not the God of Israel, who gave the Holy Land to the Hebrew people. I gave the earth to ALL humans, rather, to all creatures, to share and share alike. Palestine doesn't belong to the Jews, any more than Arabia belongs to the Arabs, or Afganistan belongs to the Taliban or Pashtun, or whomever. Besides, I didn't choose the Jews, they chose Me, because they were the first ones to see what a great thing it is to own God and have exclusive rights to Him and then do whatever you wanted to do in His name. As long, of course, as you circumcised your boys, and avoided pork and shellfish- always in My name.

Then, of course, I am NOT the Old Man with the white beard whom Michelangelo painted in the Sistine Chapel. That poor dear has since developed Alzheimer's, and is dying of old age. He took an awful blow on 9/11/01 when the greatest civilization the world has ever seen was brought to its knees by Muslim boys using America's own planes as bombs against itself- all, of course, in MY name. That's why I want nothing to do with their Allah."

"Now that we know who You are NOT, are You ready to tell us who You ARE?", I asked.

"Gladly," She said, with a smile that broke as big as a rainbow after a dismal rain.

"I am the Primal Matter of the First Explosion.

I am the Thirteen Billion Year expanding universe.

I am the Love Song of the Endless Spheres, the Gravity of the Galaxies, the Silence of the Cosmic Black Holes.

I am the churning waters of the Primeval Sea, the Rivers Running from the Clouds, the Womb of Living Brine from which all life flows.

I am Endless Evolution, marching from the Salty Sea. I am your Home which you left at birth, and the Home to which you shall return.

I am the Center of the Circle of your Sojourn.

I am Gaia, the Living Earth, and Cosmos, the Living Universe.

I am Danaos, earth mother, goddess of fertility.

I am Godde, the Soul of All reality, the Anima of Life Itself.

I am the Self Itself of the Universe.

I am the Ground of Being, the Unconscious Being underlying All That Is.

I am the All in All, the Only One, the Everything.

I am ultimate Concern, I am Love Itself.

I am all of the above and none of the above."

"Now do you know who I am?"

I was so enthralled and enchanted with her musical litany of identity, that I was in danger of taking false pride in curing her with my silly therapy.

But all I could say was, "It doesn't matter whether I know who you are, as long as I know that You know who you are. It doesn't matter whether I believe in You as long as I believe that You believe in Yourself. But it does matter that I love You, for when I love You, I become One with You and with all Being.

"In the Beginning, God made heaven and earth," and in the End was the Word, and the Word was with God, and the Word WAS God. So God had the last word like a Woman : " I am Godde."

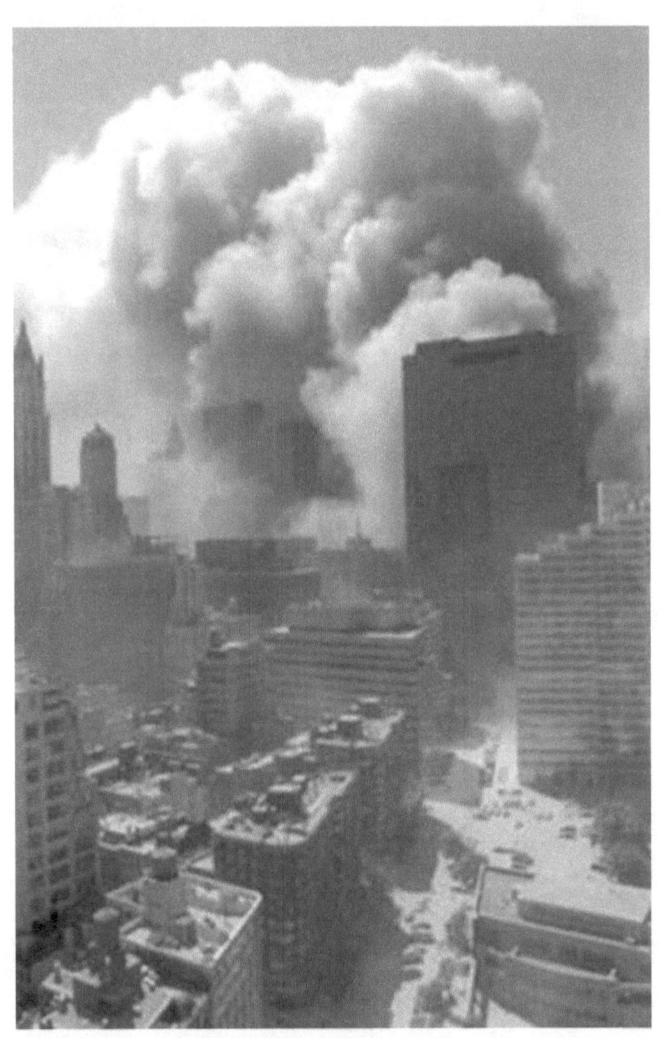

Afterword

THERAPY FOR GOD was the most delightful round of therapy that I did in 25 years of practice. I seemed to have an intense connection with God as a result of the 9/11 bombing, and the material from Her sessions came flowing out of the depths within me, with almost no effort on my part. They obviously came out of the depths of my unconscious. It took about three months to write the sessions, not quite one a week, and I shared them as they came out with about 50 relatives, friends, and acquaintances on my various E-mail address lists.

Some replied with comments and questions which went into the composition of the Preface, Introduction, Therapy Sessions, and now the Afterword. One question asked by a cousin who teaches religion to children in a Catholic parish was whether I considered myself a Christian. My answer is quite lengthy. If "Christian" means follower of Jesus, I am definitely a Christian. I believe that Jesus of Nazareth was the greatest man who ever lived. I believe that he was the closest of anyone to the incarnation of the compassion, mercy, and love which I identify with God. (This, by the way, is what Dominic Crossan of the "Jesus Seminars" says in the final analysis of his lifetime work.) In that sense, metaphorically, Jesus was the son of God, the savior of the world, the Desire of the Everlasting Hills. But if by Christian one means that I subscribe to most of what the Christian Churches officially teach about Jesus Christ, namely, that he is literally a divine person and thus son of God, that he is the Messiah, that he literally died for our sins to redeem us, that faith alone in Jesus will save us, etc., etc., no way do I believe all of that. I reject almost all the orthodox teachings of the Christian Churches which are based on the divinity of Jesus Christ. Jesus cannot be God in the sense that no one can be God. Even God is not God, if by

God you mean "A supreme Being" separate from the Universe. God IS the universe and all of us : Jesus, you, and me are part of God. None of us are separate from the One Being which is God. How can I say it any more clearly? All Being is One, All Being is Good, All Being is Beautiful.

I can just see a fundamentalist with a bumper sticker that says he just spoke to God this morning, coming up to me and saying, "What if God comes up to you and speaks to you, will you believe that God is a Person?"

No, I still won't believe God is a person, because God speaks to me all the time through my unconscious. That is the way God speaks. I am, in a sense, the voice of God who needs me to speak to myself.

But that brings up a difficult question : How can we communicate with God, if God is not a Personal God ? How can we continue to be religious if God is not a Separate Person that we can worship? Religion is meant to connect humans to God. (Re- ligio from the Latin means to "bind"), if we are already part of God, how can we be "re-bound" to God? What are synagogues, churches, mosques, and congregations supposed to be doing? I would say that religions through their various mythologies (Scriptures) connect people to the divine element within themselves, and since the divine element is within them, and they within the divine element, religious worship, ritual, scriptures, bring people into touch with their sacred and divine roots. As long as religious people understand that the divinity they are connected to can only be known metaphorically not literally. In other words, as long as they know that they are only talking to a Personal God as a metaphor for Universal Being. This is exactly what I did with my "Divine Therapy Sessions". Hopefully, I helped the reader re-connect with the hidden, unconscious, divine element within them.

This brings me to a further point. There are millions for whom religion has absolutely no appeal. Not only does religion fail to connect them to the divine element they are a part of, but actually religion drives them away from the sacred and the divine. For them, a large portion of modern society, religion has done more harm than good in the world. It has divided nations, caused wars and violence everywhere. How could this kind of religion possibly be inspired by the loving compassionate basis of reality which we reverence as God ?

A patient of mine came to me a while ago and was very upset because he could no longer gather with his extended family for the religious holidays. He said he no longer believed in religion, and could not celebrate with them, and, of course, they being religious people were very mad at him. Now this was a man who had been doing the Twelve Step Spirituality Program with AA for many years. He believed very much in a "Higher Power," and under my guidance, he was beautifully working the "Let go, let God, Go God" spirituality of AA. The first step means that one accepts one's humanity, that one's life has become uncontrollable as it does for most people with the disease of addiction. So one "let's go", that is, stops trying to control an uncontrollable life. The second step is "Let God", which means to allow the "Higher Power" of God within one to emerge and restore sanity to one's uncontrollable life. In the third step, "Go God", one simply throws oneself on the mercy and compassion of the "Higher Power" and trusts It to save one from addiction.

(Another, even simpler version of the first three steps was given to me by another one of my patients: the first step is "I can't", the second step," God can", the third step: "So I'll let Him.") This may sound overly simple, but when put into practice in the context of a support group, all of whom are practicing the same spirituality, it works. It has saved millions from life-threatening addictions over the past sixty years. With this kind of a practical, working spirituality, many people like my patient who have experienced so much negativity in organized religion can still be "religious" or bound to God.

In the therapy sessions, while I was listening to how angry God was at the orthodox of all three monotheistic religions, I thought about the difference between "orthodoxy" and "orthopraxy", which came out of the Liberation Theology movement in South America. Orthodoxy is about "correct teaching", (Greek 'ortho' for 'correct', and 'doxein' for 'to teach'),while orthopraxy is about correct practice, (Greek 'praxein' for 'to practice'.) All religions have their orthodox, who are the same as fundamentalists. They have drawn up a list of correct teachings which they get from their scriptures and traditions. They canonize or codify these teachings, and declare them to be infallible literal truths that all their followers must give intellectual assent to, under pain of death, excommunication, and damnation. Like the French in "My Fair Lady", who don't care what you do, as long as you pronounce it correctly, the orthodox don't really care how you treat other people, especially non-believers, as long as you believe the correct thing. Or as Martin Luther said, "If you sin strongly, believe even more strongly.) That is why the Vatican condemned so roundly the Latin Liberationists who railed against the conservative hierarchy for siding with the conservative rich to oppress the poor. That is why Islamic fundamentalists can kill innocents as long as terrorists believe they are martyrs for orthodoxy. That is why right- wing Christians in the U.S.A. can hate people of color, and why right wing Black Muslims can hate whites: all for very religious reasons.

I propose, instead of this tainted orthodoxy, putting the emphasis on orthopraxy, that is, the correct practice, especially the practice of charity and compassion toward others. Humans will never agree on the correct teachings or beliefs about God, but they universally agree that it is wrong to harm innocent human beings, whether they believe in God or not. The golden rule of doing to others as you would have them do unto you has been a standard of all faiths, spiritualities, religions, even atheisms since the dawn of civilization. For the three monotheistic faiths, loving God with your whole heart and soul, and your neighbor as yourself, sums up the whole law and the prophets. Terrorism would end quite soon if orthopraxy were to replace orthodoxy among the believers and non-believers alike in this world.

This brings me to my main learning experience from doing therapy for God. During the therapy sessions God was most disturbed by the fundamentalists of all religions who still cling to outmoded interpretations of their original religious myths. First of all, they seem totally unaware that the religious truths that they kill and die for are myths that cannot literally be true. These fundamentalists are threatened by anyone who would attempt to modernize their ancient myths and help them understand them in a way that works for today. They seem to be totally unaware that most of the religious truths they believe in are from an era long before the Copernican Revolution (which proved that the earth was round, and revolved around the sun.) Even further, these truths evolved before the Einsteinian Revolution of Relativity, and need to be modernized to fit into a totally different view of the universe than that of their Scripture Writers. Not only that, but the main myth of all religions: that God is the creator of the universe- needs drastic updating. If God is NOT separate from the universe, how could God create the universe? It would be absurd to think that God created himself! (We won't go into God's gender, since God is not a person, his/her/its gender is irrelevant. Just pick a gender that you can relate to and be comfortable with, in of course, a metaphorical sense.)

Apropos the myth of creation : about thirty years ago I was in conversation with my classmate, Geno McAlee, a Redemptorist scripture scholar, now deceased and definitely resting in peace, thank you. He just happened to mention that maybe God didn't create the universe, maybe matter always existed, and nobody created it. At the time, this scared me, because creation was the only proof I had for the existence of God, and if matter always existed what did we need God for ? I am sure that if I had asked Geno he would have told me that since the dawn of consciousness homo sapiens has always experienced God in his daily life. We need no proof for God's existence.

Now, after listening to God in Her therapy sessions, it is very easy for me to imagine that 13 Billion years ago there was a black hole with about a spoonful of matter so dense that it contained in compressed form all the neutrons, protons, and electrons that now compose the universe. Suddenly, there was a big bang that has been exploding now for 13 Billion years. Where did that spoonful of matter come from? Obviously, no PLACE, because there were no other WHERE'S out there. All we know is that the first moment of time began 13 Billion years ago. That big bang was the beginning of evolution. Where was God ? God was THERE ! God WAS the spoonful of matter. God was the explosion, God was the guiding power that turned the black hole into light and then 13 Billion years of evolution. God IS evolution, and as Teilhard deChardin said, "We human beings are evolution conscious of itself."

Thus we speak for God, we reveal God to Herself. We each are unique emanations of God, meant to give flesh to a particular aspect of God's infinite power, goodness, and beauty. But without our particular expressions, God remains unconscious and without voice. So each of us must pause, and center ourselves in the vast ocean of God's unconscious being and articulate what God is for each of us.

I began precisely that in the last therapy session, and I continue it now as the ending of my book, and leave it to each of you to articulate how you uniquely see God.

God is the joy of making love, the bubble of a baby's smile.

God is the tear in the toddler's eye, the prettiness of a puppy.

God is the silence of the slave, weeping to be freed, the gall of the oppressed struggling to survive.

God is compassion for the poor, the strength of the meek.

God is the hope of those who wait, the security of those who believe.

God is the freedom of the prisoner, the forgiveness of the condemned.

God is the loveliness of the leaf, the green in billowing grass.

God is the fragrance of the flower, the shelter of the trees.

God is the broadness of the plains, the snow-covered awe of mountains.

God is the blue of sky, and sun-filled clouds.

God is the acquamarine waters of the ocean, the sweep of the continents.

God is the holder of the globe, the hurler of the moon, the infinite power of suns and the breathtaking awe of planets. and their satellites.

God is the gravity of the galaxies, the force of the universe, the Strider of the Milky Way, the Fourth of July explosions of nebulae. God is the One, the True, the Good, and the Beautiful. God is the Ground of All Being, God is Ultimate concern.

GOD IS LOVE.

EPILOGUE
GOD'S FIFTEENTH THERAPY SESSION

GOD SURPRISED ME by asking for another session. Patients never come to thank me after a round of therapy. Maybe they just don't want to pay for another session, or I just don't have the time to listen to them for free. But, after all, this was Godde, Mother of All Being, so when She asked to see me again, how could I refuse ?

When She came in, I let her begin, because I was taught by my supervisors to let the patient have the first words because it was the only way to get the patient to set the aggenda. I know I have not always followed that rule, and no doubt ended up forcing the patient to talk about MY problems instead of hers.

So I let God begin.

"You ended up getting me to tell you who I am, so now I want to tell you who YOU are, and hopefully share this with everyone who reads this book, because what I say about you is equally, though uniquely, true of each of them.

"You are a spark of the original nuclear explosion. Thus you are 13 Billion years old, and you exist both in time and in the simultaneous dimension of eternity. (There is no afterlife, just a cross-over to the other dimension.)

"You are an emanation from ME, Mother of All Being. Thus you came forth in my own image and likeness, though you have no idea what that really means.

Just say you are like a child of Godde. You are like an incarnation of the Eternal Oneness of Being.

You are like an expression of the Eternal, yes, the Eternal Word made flesh.

I know it sounds an awful lot like what orthodox Christians say about Jesus Christ, but it's true. You are all Jesus Christs. You are all Abrahams. You are all Mary's, each in your own unique way.

"You are all Flower Children, all glorious blossoms of love.

"Your task is to stretch out your arms and embrace all Being with the love and compassion which I breathe into you every moment.

"I command you to heal, to forgive, especially to forgive yourself for not being everything you wish you could be, because you are already more than you could ever hope to be.

"Now go forth and do the same for others.

"Make a Garden of the earth, save my beautiful animals, and then go out and populate the planets. The only heaven is out there in the galaxies, and you are already there (and here) in the dimension of eternity.

"You are love, so go out and find someone to love, so you can go on being yourself ".

The End of The Beginning

Bibliography

Armstrong, Karen. *A History of God*. New York:Ballantine Books, 1993

Armstrong, Karen. *The Battle For .God.* New York. Ballantine Books,2000

Baum,Gregory.*ManBecoming.*New York.Herder and Herder.1971.

Berry,Thomas.*The Dream of the Earth*. San Francisco: Sierra Club Books. 1998

Buscaglia, Leo. *Love*. New York. Fawcett Books, 1972.

Davies, Paul. *God and the New Physics*. New York. A Touchstone Book, 1983

Finley, James. *Merton's Palace of Nowhere: A Search for God through Awareness of the True Self*. Notre Dame, Ind. Ave Maria Press, 1978.

Fox, Matthew. *Original Blessing: A Primer in Creation Spirituality*. Santa Fe, NM, Bear & Company, 1983.

Jaffe', Aniela. *The Myth of Meaning (According to Carl Jung's Writings). New York.* G.P. Putnam's Sons for the C.G. Jung Foundation, 1971

Miles, Jack. *God: A Biography*. New York. Random House, 1996

Miles, Jack. *Christ: A Crisis in the Life of God*. New York. Alfred A Knopf, 2001

More,Thomas. *Care of the Soul: A Guide for Cultivating Depth and Sacredness in Everyday Life*. New York. HarperCollins, 1994

Morwood, Michael. *Tomorrow's Catholic: Understanding God and Jesus in a New Millennium*. Mystic, CT. Twenty-Third Publications, 1997.

Morwood, Michael. *Is Jesus God? : Finding Our Faith*. New York. Crossroads Books, 2001

Otto,Rudolf. *Mysticism East and West*. New York. Macmillan, 1970

Progoff,Ira, *The Cloud of Unknowing: A New Translation of the Medieval Classic on Mysticism.* New York. The Julian Press, 1969

Progoff, Ira. *The Symbolic and the Real.* New York. The Julian Press

Rilke, Rainer Maria *Love Poems to God.* Translated by Anita Barrows and Joanna Macy. New York, Riverhead Books, 1996

Rubenstein, Richard, *When Jesus Became God: The Struggle to Define Christianity during the Last Days of Rome.* San Diego: Harcourt, 2000

Spong, John Shelby. *Why Christianity Must Change or Die: A Bishop Speaks to Believers in Exile.*San Francisco: HarperSanFrancisco, 1998.

Swimme, Brian. *The Universe Is a Green Dragon : A Cosmic Creation Story.* Santa Fe,N.Mex.: Bear & Company,1984

Swimme, Brian, *The Hidden Heart of the Cosmos: Humanity and the New Story.* Maryknoll,NY, Orbis Books, 1996

Swimme, Brian, and Thomas Berry.*The Universe Story: A Celebration of the Unfolding of the Cosmos.* San Francisco: HarperSanFancisco, and London: Penguin Books, 1992

About the Book

ON SEPT. 11, 2001, the therapist-author imagines God coming to him for psychotherapy after the terrorist attacks and U.S. declaration of war on terrorists. God is appalled at the violence perpetrated by religious people on both sides, in His name, since He has always been completely opposed to such absurd and pointless barbarism. Is God having a nervous breakdown, or just suffering from Post –Traumatic Stress Syndrome? From Sept.11 to December 11, God comes for therapy once a week and in the course of treatment, discovers that She is having an Identity Crisis. She realizes that the old masculine tribal God of mono-theism has been foisted on Her by the three great religions of the western world, while all spiritual people, both East and West have always experienced Her as Love. In a final surprise session, God tells the therapist who She really is and who we are.

About the Author

SAL UMANA WAS born in South Boston, MA in 1929, the year of the Crash. He attended Boston Public Latin School, then became a Redemptorist Missionary and worked in all 50 States, the Caribbean, and Italy, for 25 years. He left the clerical priest- hood to marry and for 25 more years, has practiced psychotherapy in New York as a Clinical Social Worker in English, Italian, and Spanish. God has been his best patient. (She worked with him in English.)

The Day My Ego Died

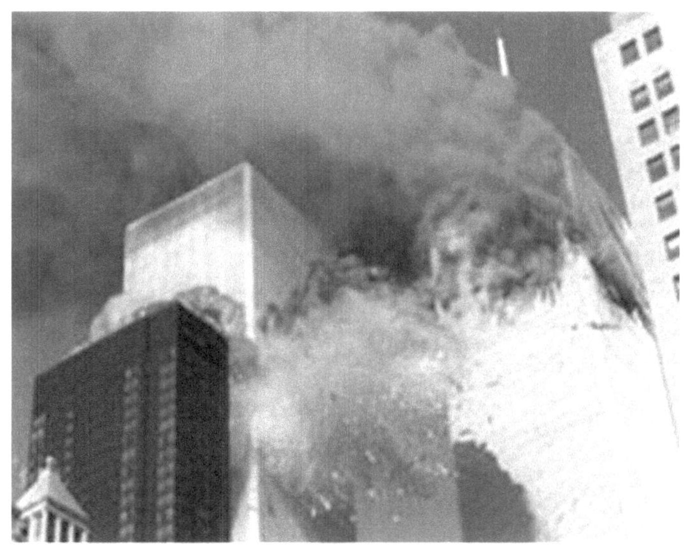

How the Twin Towers on 9/11/01 Became the Grave of My Ego

Sal Umana

O N SEPTEMBER 11, 2001, after the terrorist attacks in the name of God and the vow for vengeance in the name of the same God, the author, a psychotherapist in New York, imagines God coming to him with Post Traumatic Stress Syndrome. While in treatment with the author, God disavows any connection with the Allah of the terrorists, and the Christian crusade of the anti-terrorists. While She is at it, she denies She is the God of Abraham, either, and decides to become an atheist.

In this sequel, the author, suffering from Post Traumatic Stress Syndrome himself, returns the favor and goes to God for therapy, and ends up as a Zen Buddhist. without an Ego. God does not become a Zen Buddhist, but declares that she has never had an Ego to lose.

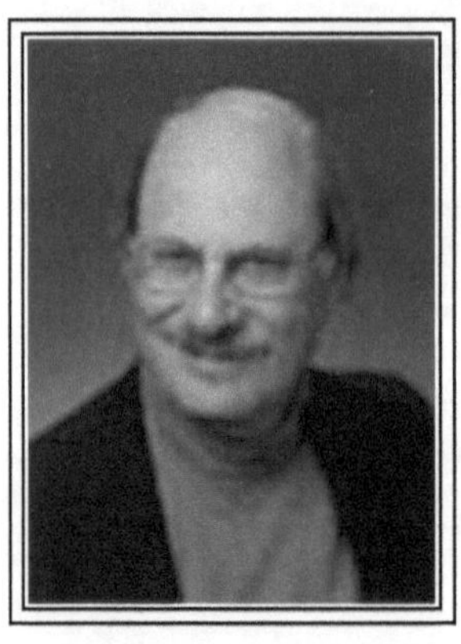

Sal Umana is a psychiatric social worker doing therapy in NY City and Long Island for 25 years. Since he had been a Catholic priest for the 25 years before that, he has managed to blend psychotherapy and spirituality into an amalgam that works for most patients, especially the addicted. He has found a blend of existential psychology, Christian mysticism, Zen Buddhism, and "Death of `Theism" Theology, that works quite well, at least on himself. The reader will find it quite helpful in negotiating the anxiety of the Age of Terrorism.

THE DAY MY EGO DIED

THE DAY MY EGO DIED:

How the Twin Towers on 9/11Became the Grave of My Ego

BY SAL UMANA

Praise for Sal Umana's first book, The Day God Died :

"I enjoyed reading *The Day God Died*. I hope it gets the hearing from the public that it deserves."- **John Shelby Spong,** author of *A New Christianity for a New World.*

"Orthodoxy spawns orthodoxy, while using God's name to justify itself. I too say that orthopraxy is the point: the reason Catholic authorities distrust both the prophet and the mystic is that both dare to hold that relating to God and not to Church rules is what makes a Christian.

"I think that your two litanies, (pp.66,77,78,80), the one defining God, the other defining us- are beautiful and inspired. Both touched me in a way that few writings do."- **Robert Willis, Ph.D.,** author of *Transcendence in Relationship: Existentialism and Psychotherapy,*

"I admire the intensity of your view of a God who is All Being and All Love. I am truly impressed when you tell God, 'The reason why You have been so depressed since Sept. 11 is that you are so disappointed at all the so-called People of Faith who pretend to speak for You, and then go against your very nature as LOVE and go out and dominate, oppress, hate, and kill, all in your Name.' **Mass. State Senator, Mario Umana.**

"I felt at home with your book. I could never have put all that you have served up into words, but I am with you 100%. I was impressed! Superb presentation! When I recently read Spong and the section on the death of Theism, I knew that I was his follower. Now I am YOUR follower. I hope more will read you so we can all be consciously with the God that is all, from all, to all, and for all." **Charles Koerber, Ph.D., Former Assistant Director of the Veterans Adminstration, Wash., DC**

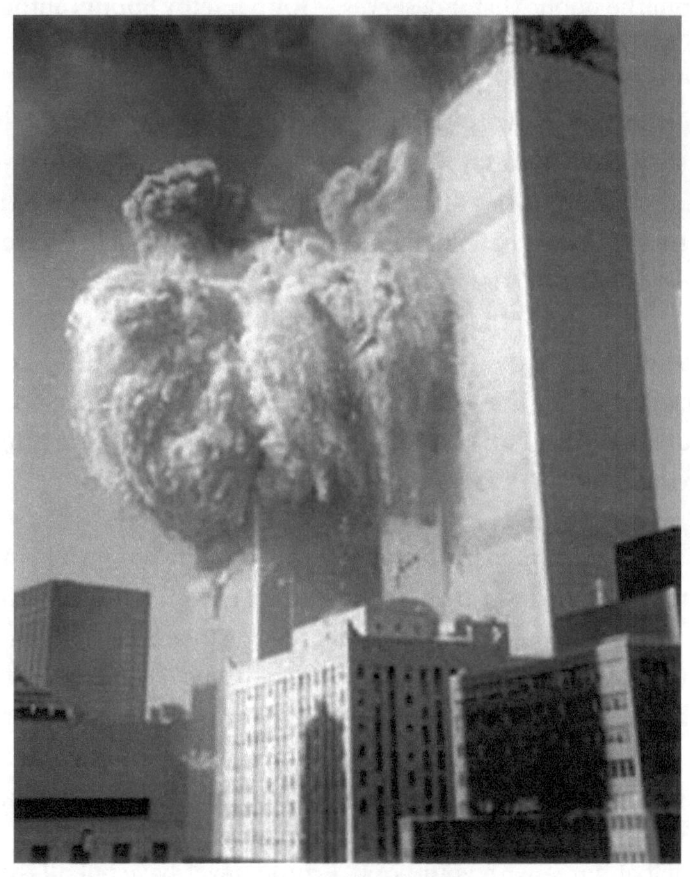

FRONTISPIECE
THE DAY MY EGO DIED

DEDICATION

To Sam O'Hara, who introduced me to John Shelby Spong

To John Shelby Spong, who taught me how to dream about a different God

To Jim Jennings who introduced me to Michael Morwood

To Michael Morwood, who taught me how to dream about the religion and spirituality of the future

To my nephew, Bob Matarese, whose Ego died years before his body

But most of all to Pierre Teilhard DeChardin, who taught me to love Our Mother Earth

Epigraph

"IF, AS A result of some interior revolution, I were to lose in succession my faith in Christ, my faith in a personal God, and my faith in spirit, I feel that I should continue to believe invincibly in the world. The world (its value, its infallibility and its goodness)- that, when all is said and done, is the first, the last, and the only thing in which I believe. It is by this faith that I live. And it is to this faith, I feel, that at the moment of death, rising above all doubts, I shall surrender myself."

TeilhardDeChardin, *Christianity and Evolution*, p.99

DeChardin was a Jesuit priest who was silenced by Rome and forbidden to write or teach any more. So he went to China to continue his work in paleontology. One morning, as the sun rose, he said Mass by holding up his hands to embrace the sun, and pronounced the sacred words of consecration over the universe of evolution, saying : "This Is MY Body!"

ACKNOWLEDGEMENTS

I WOULD LIKE TO thank everybody who stayed with me through my first book.

I thank especially the several E-mail groups who have followed me in my journey:

The former Redemptorists and present Redemptorists,

The former Movement for a Better World members,

The Umana and Castriano cousins, and the various friends and colleagues in my address book,

And finally, the twelve members of the home Mass group to which I belong.

FOREWORD
BY WILLIAM (SAMMY) O'HARA

THIS IS SAL Umana's second book, a follow up of sorts. In his first effort, *THE DAY GOD DIED*, he adroitly acted as God's therapist during the Deity's post traumatic response to the horrors of 9/11.

The result of the sessions that God underwent with her new found Therapist was a heralding of the death of the God of Theism. Sal the Therapist managed to get his patient - God - to become an atheist!

How could Sal out astonish his readers after turning God into a non-believer in Book One? Just continue on and read Sal's Opus Number Two.

In this sequel, the author, suffering from Post Traumatic Stress Syndrome himself, returns the favor and goes to God for therapy, and ends up as a Zen Buddhist, without an Ego. God does not become a Zen Buddhist, but declares that she has never had an Ego to lose.

Confusing? Well, trust Sal to take you through many sessions of therapy with God Herself as Psychotherapist. The journey takes many unexpected twists and turns. At the end, you will be called upon to decide for yourself if Sal, the patient, has been helped, not cured, by his inner self God-like therapist.

And, most importantly, you the reader will be challenged to see if your values and convictions in matters of ultimate beliefs of the Deity can stand up to a test - if you are willing to take it.

Sal is one of a long line of Catholic mystics. In fact, his novice master revealed before he died that Sal was the most mystical of all the novices he had had in twenty years at that position. All of his recent writings have been about God and isn't that the role that Mystics have always played in history?

As you read through the various therapy sessions between Sal and his alter ego, God, decide for yourself if Sal Umana is a modern day mystic.

Sal Umana was born in Boston, of Sicilian immigrant parents. After attending Boston Latin School, he gave up automatic acceptance into Harvard to go into the Redemptorist Order. After 24 years as a priest, he left and spent the next 25 years doing psychotherapy. He lives with his wife and two Shih Tzus in New York. So far, neither a Fatwah, nor an Anathema have been pronounced against him.

One thing is sure: he is determined not to leave this earthly life to discover if his musings and insights about the theistic entity he once served so faithfully throughout his life are correct before the Boston Red Sox win a World Series!

William (Sammy)O'Hara, founder of the 'Sammy' E-mail group of past and present Redemptorists, is a native Brooklynite, who along with Rudy Giulliani, is a Yankee fan. What they both don't know is that the Yankee mystique is buried at Ground Zero and will never rise again.

INTRODUCTION
HOW THE GOD OF THEISM DIED SEPT.11, BUT IS REBORN IN EACH OF US FROM THE BOOK OF TAO

THERE IS SOMETHING mysterious, without beginning, without end, that existed before the heaven and earth. Unmoving, infinite; Standing alone; never changing. It is everywhere and it is inexhaustible. It is the mother of all.

I do not know its name. If I must name it I call it Tao and I hail it as supreme. Looked for it cannot be seen; it is invisible. Listened for it cannot be heard; it is inaudible. Reached for it cannot be touched; it is intangible. These three are beyond analysis; these three are one.

The scholar needs to know more and more each day. The follower of Tao needs to know less and less each day. By inaction everything can be done. The world is won the those who leave it alone. When one feels compelled to dominate, the world is already beyond reach.

The heavens endure; the earth is very old. Why?

Because they do not exist for themselves, they therefore have long life.

The truly wise are content to be last; they are therefore first. They are indifferent to themselves; they are therefore self-confident.

Perhaps it is because they do not exist for themselves that they find complete fulfillment.

Thus, the truly wise seek Unity, they embrace oneness, and become examples for all the world. Not revealing themselves, they shine; not self-righteous, they are distinguished; not self-centered, they are famous; not seeking glory, they are leaders.

Because they are not quarrelsome no one quarrels with them. Thus it is as the ancients said: "To yield is to retain Unity" The truly wise have Unity, and the world respects them.

Tao never acts directly; it activates everything. If rulers would do likewise the world would improve of itself. But when improving, motivates Yin. Motiveless Yin is free of all desire, and being free of desire is to be serene. Being serene, the world is at peace.

The concept of Yin is ever present. It is the Mystic Female from whom the heavens and the earth originate.

Constantly, continuously, enduring always.

Use her!

In my previous book, *The Day God Died,* I discussed the Death of God as a result of the terrorist attacks of 9/11/01. By that statement, I meant that the Muslim terrorists completely discredited their deity, Allah, by perpetrating their atrocity in the name of Allah.

After that insane demonstration of perverted religious fanaticism, how can anyone ever again believe in the God the terrorists prayed to in their little Arabic religious manuals? We have become disgusted with the very idea of a God who rewards suicide bombers with Paradise and seventy five virgins for killing his own children who don't believe in Him in exactly the same way as the terrorists. There was obviously something wrong with their God as they conceived him to be.

However, the response of the anti- terrorists was even more damaging to *their* idea of God. Both Christians and Jews,in the name of their God felt perfectly justified, even obliged, to hunt down and kill the very people who,they say, call their God Father, or Allah, or All-Holy One. In other words, their God wants them to kill their other brothers and sisters in God in order to protect their own children! No wonder the atheists are having a field day laughing at them all!

Now exactly what do I mean by the "God of theism" whose grave has become Ground Zero, along with some 2800 others who lie there in Lower Manhattan.?

Theism is the teaching in traditional theology that God is a supreme being who is separate from the universe. According to postmodern theology, God is no longer separate or transcendent, but totally immanent. This means that God is within the universe not *a-part* from the universe. It might be better to say the universe is *within* God. But we are not talking about anything spacial here. God does not occupy any space. It might be better to say that God provides the Being of space or rather *Is* space. Traditionally, it was taught that God was both transcendent and immanent, that is, that God was transcendent, beyond all of the visible universe, and yet, at the same time, immanent, present within all of visible reality. That may seem like a contradiction, but because God was unlimited or infinite, He did not have to be bound by the rules of logic. However, secretly, most theists simply ignored the immanent part of traditional theism and thought of God as totally transcendental.

Now the traditional Christian theology about Jesus Christ tried to reconcile both transcendence and immanence in the person of Jesus Christ, by making him one person with both the nature of God and the nature of man. As God, he totally transcended the universe, as symbolized by his Ascension beyond the stars, and as man, he was born of woman, and therefore, immanent in the visible universe.

The problem with that was that after Jesus ascended into heaven, his humanity and immanence were largely ignored and for two thousand years he has been worshipped as the Second Person of the Holy Trinity and thus totally transcendent.

This loss of the immanence of the Second Person of the Trinity is very significant in the history of the immanent aspect of God. Humans have always had trouble dealing with the immanent aspect of their own being. Most of us are terrified by the loss of our self-conscious visible reality in the universe after death. We cannot imagine our life after death without consciousness and visibility in space and time. Thus the humanity (immanence) of Jesus Christ has largely been ignored, and he has come down to us as totally divine and transcendent.

Along with the God of Abraham and Allah, the Triune God has come down to us as a very separate, aloof and transcendent Supreme Being. Even though Jesus was proclaimed in the Gospels as "Emanuel", that is, "God-With-Us", the being with us was confined to the few years that he lived among human beings.

Shortly after Jesus' death, he became almost totally divinized by the Greco- Roman Empire until He was elevated to the status of "Christos Pancrator", "Ruler of the Universe"

When you behold the magnificent mosaics in the Byzantine Christian Domes of Monreale and Cefalu,(Sicily), and Constantinople,(now Istanbul), you understand how totally divine Jesus of Nazareth had become. True, Christian orthodoxy taught that the Second Person of the Trinity was both human and divine, and was placed at the right hand of God the Father to judge the living and the dead. But it was tacitly understood that the Second Person of the Divine Trinity was made King of the Universe, not because he was human, but because he was divine.

Now it is my hope to show that the ancient teaching about the Incarnation of Christ is really a metaphor for the deeper truth that the divine takes flesh in all of us.

To throw further light on the death of the God of theism I will try to show how this is all part of the evolution of the idea of God since the dawn of self-consciousness. Whenever *homo sapiens* first emerged, he emerged with an awareness that he was *not* God. That is, he simultaneously became aware of both life and death. While he exulted in the joy of being aware of his own being, he suffered the depression and anxiety of knowing that he would soon die. His fellow animals were neither overjoyed at the thought of being alive, nor in fear of losing life. For the other animals, living and dying was destiny. But for humans, self-consciousness naturally contained the fear of death and loss of self-conscious life. That is why man needed to project a Supreme Being who was beyond death, who would somehow rescue him from the loss of being which we emotionally experience as death.

This is where the idea of a theistic God comes from. Primitive homo sapiens needed to project an all-powerful Supreme Being, who is not subject to death, and who dwells in a "heaven" beyond the visible universe, and has the power to take us home to his heaven after we die.

Of course, man had to explain the existence of evil in the world, so he projected a God who laid down the rules and who punished evildoers with the loss of paradise, and rewarded the good with an eternal reward in His heaven.

As the theists became more sophisticated, they developed creation stories that explained the "fall" of man, and how man became corrupted and was henceforth born in "original sin". Since it was the theistic God whom man "offended" by his sins, only another God could atone for man's offenses to God. At least in the orthodox Christian way of putting it, since there can only be one God, by the theistic definition of God, then the One God had to become man to somehow atone for all sins against God.

This is where we get the Christian fundamentalist teaching: "Jesus saves". The only entrance to heaven is through the "Blood of the Sacrificial Lamb of God" who died for our sins. From the viewpoint of the 21st Century, this sacrificing and dying of God becomes not only gruesome, but nonsensical and bizarre. This, above all, since we can now see that God only became human so he could die, and as soon as he died, he went back to being anything *but* human. If brought to its ultimate conclusion, God could be accused of fraud and misrepresentation, since he was only pretending to be human. Obviously, these biblical stories of original sin and the Incarnation of Christ, and his death to atone for original sin, are myths and metaphors, and symbols.

Unfortunately, the orthodox believers have been taking these redemption stories literally for so long that the mythical and mystical meanings are obscured beyond redemption. (No pun intended!) What we really need to be redeemed from is the literal interpretation of the Scriptures *and* the rigid and dogmatic "hardening of the categories" that has set in.

For thirty years I belonged to a Religious Order which was named after the Most Holy Redeemer. Perhaps what the Order should be doing in order to be faithful to the idea of Jesus as Redeemer is to liberate the Bible and the Christian tradition from all the accretions and literal interpretations which have made much of Christian teaching so unbelievable to postmodern religious people.

Perhaps the Redemptorists should live up to their name and Redeem Jesus from his early Christian followers who made him into a Messiah he never intended to be.

Perhaps what the ancient doctrine of Redemption by the Son of God is trying to say, metaphorically, is that each of us becomes our own 'Redeemer'! Matthew Fox has written a book on "Creation Spirituality', called *Original Blessing: A Primer in Creation Spirituality.* In the reality of "Creation Spirituality", perhaps we could say that God becomes incarnate in each of us, and empowers us to atone for our own mistakes, (sins), for our own failure to continuously evolve into the emanation of God that God intends us to be.

Perhaps I am fulfilling my original vocation to follow the Redeemer by rescuing the idea of God from the literalizers who have made God into an "idol in the sky", or a kind of "heavenly Santa Claus" who is on duty all year rather than just at Christmas. I feel my mission is to turn religious teaching upside down and liberate the idea of God from an aloof separate Supreme Being to the spiritual transcendent aspect of the one visible reality of the universe.

I feel I am exalting humanity to its rightful place as the consciousness of the universe. Teilhard De Chardin, the wonderful Jesuit paleontologist who was silenced by the Vatican, back in the Fifties, was the first one to get me thinking about man being "Evolution conscious of itself." At the same time, I am honoring divinity as the transcendent life force in all of visible reality. I am saying that divinity is a necessary aspect of humanity, while at the same time, humanity is a necessary aspect of divinity. I will try in this book to prove that the theistic idea of a separate, transcendent God is a myth and symbol whose time has passed. It is very much like growing up and realizing that there is no Santa Claus.

Hopefully, this evolving of the idea of God will bring us to the beginning of the 21st Century in the development of religious consciousness. Then we will be able to discuss religion after the death of theism, and discover why those of us who have found God to be an aspect of ourselves are living a life of supreme spiritual joy.

LIBERATING CHRISTIAN TRADITION FROM THE LITERALISTS

During my Catholic Seminary years, I majored in theology for four years, enough for a Doctorate in Theology which I never received because of the Byzantine academic requirements of the Middle Atlantic States Secondary Education System.

At any rate, theology was divided into two years of Dogmatic Theology and two years of Moral Theology. The Moral Theology was mostly about the thousands of ways that people can break the Ten Commandments. It was supposed to prepare us for the ordeal of hearing confessions for the rest of our lives. But it didn't. Think of it as preparing to be the judge, the jury, and the prosecutor, all wrapped up in one, while the poor penitent was left to defend himself without a lawyer. Nonetheless, most of us found moral theology much more interesting than dogmatic theology.

In hindsight, it is easy to see why most of us did not find dogma interesting.

Dogma in Greek is the orthodox teaching of the Universal, Catholic Church throughout the past two thousand years. Most of the dogmas or teachings were "proved" from Scripture, the Councils of the Church, or the universal "magisterium" or teaching authority of the Church, which means the Pope, when he decrees infallibly "ex cathedra", i.e. from his Cathedral Seat. But it can also become dogma if all the bishops of the Church, in union with the Pope, teach it.

Most of these dogmas were learned by rote in Latin so there would be no mistake in meaning by translating them into the vernacular, and also because Latin is a dead language, and truths become canonized only when they are dead, like saints.

These dogmas were officially listed in the Latin Dogmatic Theology textbook as *"De Fide Divina"*, that is, they were of divine faith and had to be believed under pain of mortal sin and under threat of eternal damnation. This was pretty scary stuff for young men who were also taught that you could go to hell for all eternity if you had an "impure thought".

One of my Dogma Professors was nicknamed "Iggy" Everett. He somehow intuitively knew that many of the Dogmas he taught were arbitrary fabrications of the medieval Scholastics. He would joke about a Professor he had at Catholic University who told his students that he had scribbled on the margins of his lecture "argument weak, yell like hell".

Is it really fifty years since I got an A in Dogmatic Theology from Iggy Everett and my other professor of Dogma, Adam Otterbein? When they read the names of these stalwarts of sacred science, anyone who went through the seminary with me can understand why I am bedeviled by postmodern 'Death of God' Theology. Did I really spend two years memorizing all those Latin q.e.d.'s from Scripture and Scholastic Philosophy? No wonder my friends accuse me of becoming an atheist in my old age! (But, actually, now that *theism* is dead, you cannot brand those who do not believe in a theistic God as atheists. We really should be called *anti-theists*. We are not at all against God, but only against the theistic idea of God as a separate supreme being.)

Nobody ever told us that all that stuff was printed in a dead language because the God of theism was dead! Just as you can only canonize a saint when he or she is dead, so you cannot "canonize" God until He is dead. All canonization means is that this holy person is in heaven. Once the Church declares "De fide" that God is in heaven, and therefore, separate from the visible universe, they put the God of theism to death!

But all those anathemas, and condemnations to hell, if you didn't accept by rote everything that was declared "De Fide Divina"! Little did my humorous professor, Iggy Everett realize that he was referring metaphorically to the Church condemning us to hell because so many of the arguments were as weak as hell.

Anyway, I find it quite ironic that the A student in Dogma is now dedicating the rest of his life to proving that the God of Monotheism is dead, and buried in Lower Manhattan, along with about 2800 poor souls who believed in him, including the terrorists who prayed to him all night in Arabic before taking the taxi to the Boston Airport.

I remember that the early Christians were fed to the lions because they were atheists. They were not condemned for believing in Christ, but for not believing in the Roman Gods, especially the Emperor, who was the only real God who counted. Will a fatwah be put out against *ME*, or will I be declared anathema or "pereat"? ("Pereat" is Latin for "Let him go to hell!"

No, I will do what the early Christians did. They clung to their idea of God as the lions chewed away, assured that their God would give them eternal life.

So while I refuse to worship anymore the traditional God of Monotheism, I cling to my faith that divinity is the transcendence of humanity. Before my good friend, Sam O'Hara, can ask me, "What in hell do you mean by *that*?" I mean that I intuit mystically that divinity is the transcendent aspect of all reality. But especially, divinity is the transcendent side of my self. Divinity meets me in my unconscious, spiritual depths. No, there is no Santa Claus out there, there is no personal, self-conscious God out there, but there is a divine element in here, inside each of us, "In whom we live and move and have our being," as St. Paul said.

Last year, my friend, Sam O'Hara quoted Dominic Crossan as saying in a TV interview that this was the best he could come up with as to who Jesus was: Jesus was a Galilean peasant with an attitude, but that attitude was the closest any human being has ever come, to modeling the compassion of God. I add to that that Jesus intuitively perceived within himself the eternal compassion of the creative force of the universe. He spoke of this compassionate power as if it were a "Heavenly Father", because he was culturally bound to his time in the development of human consciousness. What Jesus got absolutely right was the sense that the force behind the universe is ultimately compassionate and kind, and therefore against the slaughter of innocents, the hatred of one's neighbor, and the senseless destruction and exploitation of the earth.

THE DAY MY EGO DIED

September 11, 2001 will forever remain a pivotal day in my life. It revealed to me, unconsciously and intuitively that my idea of God and my idea of myself had changed forever. These two central ideas in my life had been rapidly evolving for thirty years. When I saw the Twin Towers of the World Trade Center collapse, I knew that God and I and the universe would never be the same again.

The idea of God had to be dealt with first. So I wrote *The Day God Died*, and used the device of God's coming to me for therapy as a way of illustrating the changes in my ideas about God. I had no idea how this therapy for God would work out in practice, so I just conducted the therapy sessions as I would for any other patient.

It struck me that God, as I experienced Her, had no mind of Her own. People who read the manuscript remarked that I, the therapist, was a much more interesting character than God, the patient. Of course, I was playing both parts, but why did I give the best lines to myself as therapist? It now dawns on me that the part of God was played without self-consciousness, without Ego. My God was not very appealing or colorful, because the idea of being Ego-less and unconscious is not very appealing to me. Rather than *appealed*, I was *appalled* to realize that God was a Zen Buddhist! God was in a kind of eternal *nirvana*, totally unconscious of Herself! But why not, since God is the unconscious ground of all being, and had evolved into us so that we could provide Her with the consciousness She lacked? Hadn't I been explaining for years that the ancient doctrine of the Trinity was a metaphor for the unconsciousness of God emanating into the consciousness of man? For years, my favorite talk was on the beginning of John's Gospel as translated by J.B.Phillips (The New Testament in Modern English, Macmillan Co., NY, NY 1962).

"At the beginning, God expressed himself. That personal expression, that word, was with God and was God, and he existed with God from the beginning."

I would tirelessly explain that God the Father was a metaphor for "The Unconscious Ground of All Being", and God the Son was God's expression of himself. Now I see that all of us are sons of God, expressions of the unconscious being which is trying to reveal Itself to us and through us.

I even found a Sanskrit mantra which says almost the same thing about Ultimate Reality as the Trinity does. *Satchitananda* is made up of three words: *sat* meaning "being", *chit* meaning "knowledge", and *ananda* meaning "bliss". So the Hindus intuitively perceived that Being is unconscious of itself, but when being knows itself, through emanation, it leads to bliss, for "to know being, is to love being."

When I finished my therapy for God, it led to my own bliss, but I lost sight of the fact that God is still unconscious being. God is infinitely blissful, even though She remains unaware, and totally un-self- conscious. Which brings us back to God as a Zen Buddhist in a state of *nirvana*.

Something was tugging at the depths of my self-consciousness, in the twilight zone where it meets the unconscious.

GOD BECOMES MY THERAPIST

(How God's therapist ended up
with God as *his* therapist.)

MY FIRST THERAPY SESSION WITH GOD

I T HAD BEEN a year since I finished doing a series of therapy sessions for God, and I was feeling the need for some therapy myself. The world was still languishing in a global war on terrorism, and everybody was rolling up his or her sleeves to get a smallpox vaccination. People who work in the skyscrapers of Manhattan were buying parachutes which were automatically set to work anywhere above the fifteenth floor. (Nobody bothered to explain that they only worked on the side of your building where there were no lower buildings to fall into. But then, again, perhaps they will give courses on how to float on your parachute to a safe heaven. Did I really say "heaven", instead of "haven.?"

The American Empire of George Bush II was well on its way to being established in Europe, Africa, and Asia. Bush's brilliant war on Iraq was proceeding almost flawlessly and American Petroleum was in place to ensure two SUV's in every suburban driveway in all fifty United States. I had buried the God of Monotheism at Ground Zero, and had finished a book on the subject which nobody ever understood, and I was feeling the usual depression I get after any of my major failures in life.

I turned to what was left of my idea of God and asked her to take me on as a patient.

"Why are you coming to *ME*?" She asked. "Didn't you just write a book proving that I'm dead?"

"No, I didn't! I just said that the God of theism is dead!"(Why do I suddenly start shouting when God accuses me of something I did or did not do?)

"The God of Theism is who I used to be?" She shouted, proving that we both can shout.

"No, not exactly," I said. "The God of Theism is really a very primitive idea of God that goes back to the tribal gods of the Middle East, and to Greek, Roman, and Teutonic mythology. They were really idols made up by various tribes and later promoted to the universal, one God of monotheism, who doesn't exist either!"

"So who am I? ' God asked querulously?"

"I told you in your therapy sessions! You are not a Separate Supreme Being, rather, you are the Ground of All Being!"

"So I'm not a separate person in my own right? I'm not even a 'Multiple Personality Disorder' like the Father, Son, and Holy Spirit, three persons in one?

"No to the first question, no to the second, and no to the third", I answered

"Then why are you talking to me, if I am not a person? And how can I talk to you if I am not a person?"

"I am talking to whoever, or whatever You are", I said, wondering if I was losing my mind.

"What in hell or heaven is that supposed to mean? Are you trying to say that you are talking to yourself and listening to yourself? All at the exact same time?"

"Bare with me awhile!" (Again the shouting). "This is just a literary device, in which the writer expresses his thoughts by inventing an imaginary character to talk to and listen to!"

"Beautiful! A real person would know that anyone who talks to himself is whacko!"

She wasn't going to make this easy for me. Perhaps I had come down too hard on the *Death of God* theme, and now She was getting back at me.

"I already told you that *you are not dead*, just the God of Monotheism is dead! "Can't you get that through your head? (Sorry, you don't have a head, do you?)You still exist but I need to work on a new understanding of who you are or what you are!"

"Okay, let me see if I have this straight. I am what's left of your idea of God after the God of Monotheism died".

"Something like that, but I don't know what to do with whatever God now is." At least the shouting had stopped.

"So instead of the old all-powerful, all- knowing '*guy in the sky with the pie*', I have become a *literary construct*?"

"Just for the purposes of these therapy sessions!" (Somehow I was back to shouting). "I have some new ideas of who you are: like You are the transcendent aspect of reality, You are the divine aspect of myself."

"You got to be kidding! Now God has become part of *YOU*?"

"I know that sounds crazy, but that seems to be the choice that God has made. God has allowed us to define Him and name Him! Remember in the Bible, in the book of Genesis, God tells man to name all the animals, thus signifying that man has dominion over all the earth? Well, I believe that God somehow has asked us to name Him, and thus God gives us dominion over Himself, or rather God signifies that He is part of our Self, and we are part of His Self."

"I must be a very crazy God to do that. What you are saying is that I need you to know who I am."

"What I am saying is that I believe you have chosen to do precisely that. You, God, have chosen to need me."

"So I have chosen to let you decide Who I am, and you want to come to therapy to *ME* to find out who *You* are? See you next week."

And she stormed out of the session in a very ugly mood.

My Second Therapy Session with God

In preparing for my second therapy session, I had a few seemingly insurmountable problems. First of all, I didn't know if I had a therapist. Secondly, my therapist, if I had one, had no idea who *SHE* was, so how could She tell me who *I* was? Thirdly, I had such a terrible transference problem with her that I wasn't sure if I could work with Her at all. Finally, She had such a monumental *COUNTER- TRANSFERENCE* problem with me, that I didn't think she would be able to work with me!

"Hello!" I heard a sharply inflected voice making a four syllable word out of 'hello'.

"Okay," I said, "Have you decided to be my therapist?"

"Only if you stop yelling at me. You are very disrespectful. After all, if you are right, then I'm God, and I should be treated with a lot more respect."

"But you are part of me, and I am part of you, so I can yell at myself."

"No you can't. That is a very lame excuse. You can't disrespect yourself or anyone else in the universe. But especially, you can't disrespect *ME*!"

"Well, you yell at me all the time." "But that is only a reaction to your yelling at *ME*. It's all transference and counter-transference stuff going on all the time between you and *ME*."

I felt sufficiently rebuked. "Are you through laying down the rules for our therapy sessions, or do you have some other rules and regulations, or should I say *COMMANDMENTS*, for me?"

"You see what I mean? There's no excuse for snapping at me like that. You have always had a problem with authority of any kind and you see red any time anyone tries to make rules or regulations for you to obey. George Gearty, your Dean in the first year of the seminary told you that." "Okay, so I have always been a rebel and an anarchist!" (At least I wasn't shouting, well not too loud). "Is this a problem that you are going to treat in my therapy?"

"If you want me to."

"But I have much more serious problems than adolescent counter- dependency."

"You can say that again!" my divine therapist said, jumping at a chance to put me in my place. "But before we get into the myriad things that are wrong with you, I would like to make a few things clear about our relationship".

"Like what?"

"First of all, don't call me your therapist. You are your own therapist here. Since I am not a separate person from you, but only the Ground of your being, you are really only talking to yourself."

"You mean I am doing what Freud did: a self-analysis?"

"That's right, and Jung says that he broke with Freud because Freud lied about his self-analysis. Jung published a letter in which Freud tells him that he could not tell the truth about his, (Freud's), own dreams, because he would have lost all of his authority as a leader of modern psychology."

"But I don't have any authority to lose".

"To repeat a phrase I used before, you can say that again. But I am not talking about your losing your non-existent authority. I am talking about the danger of self-analysis. You know how many therapies go wrong, even when the therapist is in supervision. In your case, you have neither a therapist nor a therapist-supervisor."

"That may be so, but I have God to help me. 'I will abide,-with God at my side!'", I kidded Her.

"You know, you are beginning to sound like a Theist again. For a minute there, I thought I was listening to the Pope.

"Think about this, and I'll see you next week."

My Third Therapy Session with God

I couldn't wait to get going in my next session, after being so roundly clobbered by God in my previous session.

"So you were trying to tell me that I am my own therapist, and that this is self- analysis", I began.

"You are starting to get it right", God said.

"But who is taking the part of God in this self-analysis?" I asked. My head was starting to spin slightly. This could get very confusing.

"You are taking the part of God, and you are taking the part of yourself," God replied.

"But which part of me is playing myself, and which part of me is playing God? What am I a schizophrenic, or a multiple personality disorder?"

"There *ARE* no parts to you. You are one person talking to yourself. But, as a mystic, you happen to have some kind of special hotline to your unconscious, where you seem to get messages from the 'divine' side of your personality, from the supernatural, spiritual depths of yourself."

"Sounds a lot like all those crazy cell- phone users running around. How lonely can they be? Why I saw a guy at the gym the other day talking to someone on the phone while he was taking a shower! Am I as screwed up as they are?"

"I don't know how 'screwed up' they are, but let them come to therapy and we'll see what we can do to help them. As for you, you have this ability to access your unconscious. It's good, but should be compared to what other people are hearing from their unconscious. Eventually it will all pan out into something most enlightened human beings can subscribe to."

"So for the purposes of this self- analysis, can I call my special hotline to the unconscious, God?"

"Not exactly," God said. "You can use the word 'God' for that other message you hear, but do not for a moment try to equate it with some divine person. Let's just say, 'A voice from your unconscious, which you call God just to have a convenient label.'"

"Enough already with the divine cell- phone!" (Okay, I yelled, but I was getting exasperated with her diversions and circumlocutions). "I've got some serious problems here to deal with! You said yourself that I was 'seriously screwed up.' Are you talking 'certifiably insane' here"?

"No, I'm not saying you are mentally ill, but you have an awful lot of problems that prevent you from being a happy human being."

"Good! That is what I wanted to hear you say. Since I am not crazy, then we can deal with some serious problems I have with life, human nature, death, life after death, and so on."

"But wait," God said, "I can't help you with the big questions about life and the universe, until you can deal with the little questions about yourself and your own life."

"What are you talking about?"

Now God was in Her own element. "I am talking about people like you who have all kinds of philosophical, theological, spiritual, and religious questions, and you are desperately looking for answers, but you are never going to hear the answers, or even understand the answers when you hear them, because you are so bogged down with emotional, psychosexual, and psychological problems."

"Now I know you must be God, because only God could come up with such a convoluted sentence!" (But I didn't yell).

"Freud did some interesting work on the psychological origins of religious sensibility, but you Catholics never paid any attention to him because you had your own dogmas proclaiming that faith is a gift from God and had nothing to do with emotional or psychological needs."

"You are getting very heavy on me again. And besides, you said, 'You Catholics', and I am not a Catholic anymore, but I always thought God was a Catholic."

"I only seem to be obtuse to you because you are afraid to admit that you don't have it all together after 74 years of living. You are definitely not 'together' in the sense that they meant it in the 60's drug culture. If you recall, 'together' comes from 'getting your shit together'. The drug addict finally knew that he was in recovery when he stopped having bouts with diarrhea. You are not 'together' because you have not yet recovered from your addiction to feeling good."

"But", I asked, "does that make me mentally ill because I am addicted to feeling good?"

"I just told you, you are not mentally ill, at least you are not ill enough to get an insurance company to pay for your treatment."

"You mean I can't charge Medicare and AARP Supplemental Insurance for these sessions? Just kidding! I know you don't have a license to do therapy in New York State, and you definitely are not part of Medicare and AARP's network of providers!"

With that, my divine therapist left in a monumental huff, like the Diva She is, without even taking a curtain call."

MY FOURTH THERAPY SESSION WITH GOD

Since my divine therapist had dropped a bomb on me in my last session, I couldn't wait to confront her again.

"So you think I am addicted to feeling good?" I asked.

"I thought I would get a rise out of you with that one."

"Well, you know what I think? I think you are projecting your own problem on to me. It's called counter-transference when the therapist has his/her own problems and unconsciously projects them on to the patient."

"What problem am I projecting on to you?" She asked. " And anyway, didn't you say that everything I do is unconscious.?"

"This stuff about being addicted to feeling good. *YOU* are the feel good God who prides yourself on being full of fun all the time. 'God's in His heaven and all's well with the world.' You have the poets and the hymn writers all extolling you as number one Santa Claus of the universe. If anybody is addicted to feeling good, it's You!" (Notice, I am not shouting. Just being calm and collected. That's when I know I'm right."

God was not pleased. "The poem should now say 'God's in *Her* heaven'! Do you realize what you are doing now? You are taking the part of the therapist and trying to analyze your analyst! Don't you see how crazy this is becoming? First you try to get *ME* to be your therapist, and then you try to analyze *ME*! You have invented a totally new ANAL analysis. What shall we call it, 'anal-ysis'? But so far your 'anal-ysis' of yourself smells as the root word would imply."

"Maybe I'm inventing a new form of therapy, in which the therapist and the patient analyze each other."

"You don't even know how to do the old form of therapy, how are you going to invent a new one? After all, since Freud, who published his book on dreams in 1903, you have a hundred years of analysis to learn from. So just go back to being the patient and let *ME* analyze you. Enough with the smart aleck remarks about you therapist's counter-transference. If I need any help with my counter-transference, I'll see a supervising therapist, and I'm telling you right now, it definitely won't be *you*!"

"Okay, okay," I answered, "So the thing about you being addicted to feeling good was just a ploy to avoid looking at my own problem with depression and anxiety."

"It was a very crude attempt to put up a smokescreen so you can remain in denial about your depression." God was really becoming animated. "It is so ironic that you blamed *ME* for my 'feel good' euphoria, when you are the one who is addicted to feeling good. Why are you so afraid of your underlying depression? Why can't you accept that being human means being depressed and anxious?"

"Why does human equal depressed and anxious?" I had to ask Her.

"Just think about it for a moment. You are but a handful of molecules, sitting on a speck of dust, orbiting a below average star at the end of a very small galaxy that is 100,000 light years across. It can be very depressing to be that insignificant, if you let it get to you. But add to your insignificance the precariousness of your position. You have no idea where you came from, or where you are going. At any moment, your truly insignificant life can end. If you are not anxious and scared, then you are in denial, and just don't get it."

"This sounds terribly hopeless," I said. "Well," She said, "like everything else in life, you have to accept reality as you find it. What other choice do you have? As hard as the truth is to accept, it is always better than whatever is in second place. And don't you clever little humans have a million lies to live, before you come down to accepting the truth about yourselves?"

"Wow! You are making this too grim!"

Now that God knew that she had my attention, she could proceed, (with caution, of course, since I am only human). "You are a typical human, in that you spend your whole life pursuing the million lies about yourself, rather than the one truth about yourself that I am giving you now, namely, that being human is naturally depressing and anxiety provoking.

"Take depression for example. Depression comes from a feeling of loss. Humans are born with a feeling of loss, something like 'Paradise Lost' that the poet Milton wrote about. You have this feeling of emptiness and incompleteness. You have a self-consciousness as big as the universe, and at the same time you are aware of your insignificance and precariousness *vis a vis* the rest of the universe. You have this feeling of being cheated. Somehow you have been deprived of your rights. You want to live forever, and yet you are not even sure of the next hour. This is very anxiety provoking."

God was not giving me a prescription for feeling good about myself. "So what am I supposed to do?"

"The first thing you have to do is face the truth about yourself. Accept the fact of your own insignificance, emotionally. By that I mean, be true to your inner feelings of depression and anxiety. Maybe intellectually, or intuitively, or spiritually you have some sense that you are more than a string of DNA on a very tiny planet. But emotionally, that is, in your gut, you have this sinking feeling of loss, and anxiety, and depression. Emotionally, you have to learn to mourn that loss that you feel. It is not unlike mourning for a loved one who has passed away. You start with gratitude for having known the loved one, and you end with acceptance of life without him or her. In your case you learn how to be grateful for the gift of existence, and then how to accept all of its limitations."

"Does the depression ever go away?" "Not exactly. But the more you accept it, the more easily you learn to live with it as a permanent part of the human condition. It's like the 'Terrible Beauty' of the poet that is integral to all human tragedy."

"I need to talk about this a lot more." "Sorry," God said, "I hate to be the bearer of bad news, but it's about time you started facing reality about yourself and the human condition." And with that she disappeared into an emptiness as big as the universe.

My Fifth Therapy Session with God

God had surely intended me to ponder the infinite depths of the existential, nihilistic questions She posed, *a la* Jean Paul Sartre. And ponder them I did for hour after hour. She was the one, presumably, who had created this nihilistic situation. Was she trying to tell me that there was some vast eternal plan in all of this, *a la FIDDLER ON THE ROOF*?

I couldn't wait to tell her this in my fifth therapy session.

"You are asking a whole bunch of philosophical and theological questions," She read my mind. "They have no place in psychotherapy. If you want me to answer these questions, you'll have to write another book, making me your philosopher or theologian. Right now, you will have to stick to your own personal analysis. I have already told you that you have got to accept the fact that you are an extremely insignificant, limited, clueless little animal on a below average planet on the cheap end of a mediocre galaxy".

"In other words, you are telling me that I am not God! You sound like Chevy Chase on *Saturday Night Live*, 'Good Evening, I'm God and you're not!'"

"Again, that's a philosophical barb, save it for your book on philosophy. But analytically speaking, how are you dealing with the depression and anxiety that naturally flows from being aware of yourself as being born on this planet?"

"I feel like Charley Brown when he goes to Lucy for his five cents worth of psychotherapy. Charley tells Lucy that he feels like he doesn't belong. Lucy says everybody feels like he doesn't belong somewhere. 'So where do you feel you don't belong, Charley Brown?' And Charley answers, 'Earth!'

"It doesn't feel good at all. It has been a miserable week worrying about it."

God was waiting for this chance. "And you spent most of the time intellectualizing yourself out of it with all those questions about God maybe having some eternal plan for you. Again, I take you back to your father, Freud. Everybody has that feeling that he doesn't belong.

Freud says nobody wants to be born. All human beings come out of the womb terrified. After nine months of living in the luxury hotel of the womb, they are thrown out into the cold cruel world and they're so depressed they start to cry, and some of them never stop whining until they die."

I returned to my favorite Ego psychologist, Erick Erickson. "Or as Erickson says, the first task we have is Trust vs Mistrust. How can we learn to trust life when we are expelled from the womb so violently, and immediately feel the contrast in the world outside the womb? No wonder so many people spend their lives desperately trying to recapture the insouciance of the womb. Do you think the people who invented Prosac had that in mind?"

God was in her element, "And here, if you want to get theological, is where your father Freud comes in and says humans are so depressed and anxious and faced with annihilation that they invent the Father God of the monotheistic religions. So Freud went and dumped the Father God as a projection coming out of human needs, and in place of religion he gave you 'voila': *psycho-analysis*. Freud even fancied himself to be the Messiah that the Jews had been waiting for, who would inaugurate a new age of freedom of the soul, where you would be in possession of yourselves and reasonably happy 'loving and working' and then sleep in peace forever. And of course after 25 years of doing analysis, you now know for sure that it takes more faith to believe that analysis will cure you than it ever did to believe religion will cure you."

"So now I'm stuck without God the Father, and without Freud the Messiah".

My Sixth Therapy Session with God

I wasted no time at all in getting in to my sixth therapy session. I was still smarting from the re-hashing of an old paper I wrote about the dishonesty of psychoanalysis. Freud had thrown out God, and put himself in God's place. He had discarded religion and enthroned his own psychobabble in its place.

"First you tell me that I have to save my philosophical questions for another book, and then you go into a whole series of philosophical and theological questions about Freud. Can we get back to my depression and anxiety?"

"Are you talking about your existential depression or your emotional depression?" God quipped.

"What's the difference?"

"Prosac doesn't cure existential depression."

"But how do I know which one I have?" I asked my therapist.

"Take Prosac, and if your depression doesn't go away, then it's existential. (Just kidding)."

"That's not funny. Are you saying if I have existential depression I need to see a philosopher instead of a psychotherapist?

Why don't you just listen to me and tell me what I'm suffering from?"

"I'm your therapist, at this moment, not your God. Even though many doctors *THINK* they are God, I who really *AM* God don't think of myself as infallible. Therapists should mostly ask questions, and never, ever give answers."

"Talk about a philosophical question? Can't we get back to my therapy?" I quipped.

"I'm sorry. How can I help you?" God asked.

"You pointed out that I have an underlying depression, and you're right. I don't care if it's psychological, emotional, intellectual, philosophical or theological. It hurts and it's messing up my life. As a matter of fact, I'm killing myself trying to escape depression. You got any idea how tiring it is for an old guy like me to run around like crazy just to keep busy? If I don't kill myself skiing on the slopes, or get a heart attack playing tennis, I'm going to bore myself to death going to absolutely abominable movies, and plays. I fall asleep watching football, hockey, and baseball on TV, where all these idiot millionaires play worse than the kids on the street. Then, in the summertime, I walk five hours, three times a week on the golf course, making an absolute fool of myself with a crooked stick designed to miss the ball by inches. Thank God I am not like so many other Americans who are drinking themselves to death, or drugging themselves, or smoking, eating, themselves to death. Not to mention all the ones on caffeine or doped up on anti-depressant medications by their psychiatrists. Or the ones who are just addicted to sex and overdosing on Viagra. At least they are getting a bang for their bucks, while all I am doing is running out of energy and boring myself to death."

God said, "Think of the people who are dying of cancer. What so many of them have discovered is that they have to focus on what they have right now in being alive. Instead of going crazy trying to enjoy as much of life as they can before they die, they must learn to appreciate one moment of time. Again, it's like I said about mourning the loss of a loved one. You have to think of all the things you appreciated about life, find something in just one moment of time that can be eternal if you really give yourself to it. And all of a sudden, you see a terrible beauty in the moment. Instead of running away trying to escape from the thought of death, and the feeling of loss, you grieve for the beauty of what you are losing, and you weep for the exquisite feeling of gratitude for having been alive at all."

I had to show God how smart I was. "Isn't that what Kuhbler-Ross says in her five steps of accepting death?"

God went on. "She goes beyond simple gratitude for having been alive. For her, facing death means facing the denial that most humans have about death. Ernest Becker wrote a Pulitzer Prize winning book *THE DENIAL OF DEATH*, in which he points out that most human beings spend their entire lives in neurotic or psychotic denial of death. In fact humans cannot go for even one hour admitting to themselves that they are actually going to die. It is impossible to live for more than a moment with the full knowledge that you are going to die. Even dying people who have just accepted death will immediately go back to talking about what they are going to do when they get home from the hospital. But when the iron curtain of denial begins to crack, they see the tremendous burning anger seeping through that finally eats a hole in the curtain. Then after hiding behind the curtain again with a bout of bargaining, like 'maybe I won't die right away, maybe somehow I can avert death.' Finally, the iron curtain drops for good, and they are in depression. That means they have stopped denying death, at least for the moment."

I couldn't resist another barb at the divine therapist. "Is that neurotic depression or existential depression?"

She surprised me and said, "If it's in your heart, it's neurotic depression; if it's in your head, it's existential depression."

"I thought you said that therapists are only supposed to ask questions?"

"Not when the patient already knows the answer. See you next week."

MY SEVENTH THERAPY SESSION WITH GOD

In preparing for my seventh therapy session, I wondered if I had heard God correctly. Was She trying to tell me that life is more about death than it is about life? That joy is more about accepting sorrow than it is about having a good time? That depression can only be overcome by learning to live with loss and deprivation? That fulfillment is more about emptying yourself, and that denial is trumped by the truth every time?

"God, are you there?, I asked.

"What kind of a question is that?," She asked indignantly, "You know I am always here!"

"I meant, are you there to begin another therapy session?"

"That is entirely up to you, since we have already established that you are doing self-analysis here."

"Enough already," I (almost) shouted. "Are you trying to tell me in this treatment of depression you are conducting, that sorrow must be my 'Lady Lover', like St. Francis with his 'Lady Poverty', and like Dante with his lady lover 'Beatrice' or 'Beatific Vision'?"

"As a matter of fact, I am,"God said. "Francis of Assisi and Dante Alighieri were brought up in the Troubadour tradition. They idealized platonic love, as symbolized by a beautiful lady. Love was like the Holy Grail for the medieval romantic. For Francis, dedicating himself to Lady Poverty was his way of literally following the words of Jesus, 'Go, sell all that you have and give it to the poor, and come follow me.' Francis was the first one who took the gospels literally: that it is impossible for a rich person to save his soul. 'For what does it profit if you gain the whole world and lose yourself?' For years, the rich and powerful had tried to explain away the stark words of the original Gospel by saying that Jesus was only talking about spiritual poverty, not actual physical poverty. The famous passage where Jesus says that it is easier for a camel to pass through the eye of a needle, than for a rich person to enter the

Kingdom of God, was interpreted metaphorically. They said that the 'Eye of a Needle' was a very narrow passageway on the trail going up from Jericho to Jerusalem where you had to strip a loaded camel to squeeze him through the narrow rock opening. But the joke is, that even if Jesus was actually talking abut *THAT* 'Eye of a Needle' it would mean even more that the rich must strip themselves of their possessions before they could get into the Kingdom of God! Francis was the first one who understood literally that *ANY* attachments to material goods are going to prevent you from being spiritually rich. Again, the joke there was that as soon as Francis died, his followers collected all the money they could beg, and built themselves convents. Enough with the life of a wandering mendicant like Jesus or Francis."

"So," I said, "if St. Francis's lady poverty was turned into a whore after his death, and the Franciscan 'beggars' became pimps, what happens to my 'Lady Sorrow' as the solution for depression?"

"This 'Lady Sorrow' is a metaphor for depression itself. You must accept depression; love her, live with her. Do not abandon her as you have been doing, running off to golf, driving for hours to the slopes. Learn to live with your bride Depression. You will find that your love for her grows. Depression is about the tragedy of the human condition. It binds you together with the rest of humanity."

"Something like St. Francis' embracing of emptiness led him to fullness?" I asked.

"Yes, your embrace of Depression will lead you to joy. St. Francis' life and work was one long paradox. The man with no earthly goods was sent to teach the Catholic Church that it did not need goods. So ironic that Francis went to Rome to ask permission to found an Order of Beggars, and the Pope had a vision of this homeless man from Assisi holding up the Church."

"Yes," I said, "I remember when I was in Rome, standing at the end of the piazza of St. John Lateran where they have a statue of St. Francis reaching up with both hands toward the Basilica of St. John at the end of the square and holding it up with his frail arms."

"Of course," God went on "the Church never gave up its wealth, and went on to cause the Reformation by scandalizing the rest of Europe with its corruption and riches. How ironic today that the Catholic Church is finally facing bankruptcy because it may have to give up most of its wealth in payment to victims of sexual abuse. Maybe the Catholic Church will finally follow the Gospel of Jesus, sell all that it has, and follow Jesus into the Kingdom of God."

"But it is very important," I said, "that the Church recognize that the God of the Gospels be re-understood."

"Let the Church read your book on the death of the God of Monotheism. Right now, we have to get back to your 'Lady Depression', as Francis of Assisi went back to Lady Poverty. Francis is famous for his paradoxes: love in place of hate, joy in place of sorrow, eternal life in place of death. Let's answer the questions you were wondering about at the beginning of this session. For you, life is to be found in embracing death rather than in dreaming of paradise. Joy is to be found in sorrow rather than in having a good time. Depression is finally overcome by accepting loss and deprivation. Give up all your denial and accept the truth about yourself, and about the universe, and it will make you free."

My Eighth Therapy Session with God

I could not stop worrying about what She had left me with: the truth will make me free? When she showed up for my eighth session, I was worn out thinking about truth and freedom.

I followed my traditional therapy rules, and let myself speak first, as the patient. "You said the truth would make me free, but I feel like I am in solitary confinement. What is the truth that will make me free?"

"I told you at the end of the last session: the truth about yourself and the truth about the universe," God answered.

"Why do I have to know the truth about the universe? Can't I just find out the truth about myself?"

"The truth about *YOURSELF* is the truth about the universe."

"Oh, oh!" I shouted like a fool, "Here we go again! And of course, the truth about me and the universe is also the truth about God."

"Please leave *ME* out of this! However, the truth is that your truth and my truth, and, of course, the universe's truth are one. All truth is one as the Greek philosophers said. 'All being is one, all being is good, all being is true.'"

"And I remember my poetry teacher, Father John Duffy, wrote his doctoral dissertation on 'All being is beautiful.'"

"Are we going to get into the question of identity? Does knowing the truth about myself mean the same as knowing who I am?"

God said, "Only in so far as identity means you must identify with the universe. That is essentially all the identity you need. As *DESIDERATA* says, 'You are a child of the universe, you have a right to be here, no less than the sun, and the moon, and the stars.'"

"Is that all I am: 'A child of the universe?' Where is the uniqueness in that?"

God answered in a deep meditation, "Don't be so hung up on who you are, as opposed to everyone and everything else in the universe. Besides, *who* you are, and *what* you are, are two entirely different concepts."

"Say what?" I asked in my best ebonics.

"Who you are refers to your ego as a separate center of consciousness. It is a combination of millions of years of genetic inheritance combined with your own lifetime of decisions for better and for worse. To that conglomerate of genes, and decisions, we give a name: Sal Umana. But essentially this unique *you* is a figment of your own imagination."

"But didn't we sing in the Marriage Encounter Movement, 'Yes I know I'll never find another you?'"

"Oh, that's a lovely romantic idea that's been foisted on you by this adolescent pop culture, begging for esteem, whining immaturely to know your unique identity."

"But," I said, "look at all the cemeteries and burial places that go back through the pyramids to the very beginning of 'homo sapiens'. It has always meant a great deal to humans to have their bones neatly buried with their names on them."

"Yes", God admitted, "Mankind has always yearned for immortality and has always wanted to keep his own unique identity forever, but look at *Me*, do I wonder about *My* identity? Do I care *Who* I am? It's not an accident that no one has ever discovered the identity of God. Nobody ever has, and nobody ever will, because I don't know who I am either. So why do you care who *You* are?

"Now *What* you are- that is a different story. What I am, what you are, what the universe is. That is what matters. That is the only identity that you should care about. 'You are a child of the universe.' You are, as Teilhard DeChardin said, 'Evolution conscious of itself'. That's what you are!"

"And what are you?", I asked Her.

"I am the ground of all being. I am the universe. I am evolution itself.

"And you are my voice."

"If that is the truth about me", I said, "Then it should set me free."

"And if it doesn't set you free, it is not the truth."

Like St. Exupery's *Little Prince*, I repeated, "And if it doesn't set me free, it is not the truth."

MY NINTH THERAPY SESSION WITH GOD

My therapist had left me with a heavy burden to contemplate during the week. It was the truth of *what* I am as opposed to the truth of *who* I am? And this truth about what I am will set me free? It was a long wait until I could lay my questions on her.

"You said that the truth about what I am will set me free? But how do I know if it's the truth?"

"If it sets you free," She said.

"But how do I know if I'm free? This sounds so much like the psychedelic platitudes of the 60's. It sounds like Flower Children in Haight-Ashbury, high on weed, or acid, telling us to 'Let it all hang out.'"

"Freedom goes back a long way," God said. "Your country is based on life, liberty, and the pursuit of happiness, but I am sorry to say, your founding fathers were not really free. If they had been free, they would not have had to enslave others. Freedom is like love, you lose it if you don't give it away. The founding fathers believed in freedom for themselves, not for anyone else. And the ruling class of the United States has always, to this very day kept the lower classes oppressed."

I couldn't help myself. "You mean the founding fathers were not unlike the Republicans of today?"

God said, "I will answer that only to say that I am sick of people saying 'God is on my side' I don't take sides, especially partisan political sides. Just remember that your national anthem sings of 'The land of the free and the home of the brave.'"

"Are you saying that I will know I am free if I am brave? Sounds like the conservatives again!"

"I regret that you are too old to be drafted," She said, sarcastically. "You will know that you are free if you are in possession of yourself!"

Did I detect the beginning of a shout? "What does possession of myself mean?"

Now that She had a captive audience, She began, "You are in possession of yourself when you can take full responsibility for yourself, when you stop blaming God, your parents, your teachers, your past, your present, or your future. It's also called 'growing up'. All of a sudden, you wake up in the eternal now. You have no past and no future. You belong to no one but yourself, yet you suddenly are responsible for everything else and everyone else. But there's not a damn thing you can do about anything or anybody, especially yourself!"

"But that's crazy!" I wanted to shout, but only said half-loud. "Are you saying that I am crazy? 'Cause that is how I feel!"

God did not answer.

"I'm sorry," I pleaded with Her, "I just can't seem to grasp the contradiction. You are saying that I must accept responsibility for everything and at the same time accept the fact that there is nothing I can do to fulfill that responsibility?"

"That's right. Now you know how *I* feel! Now we are getting into the essence of freedom.

"You mentioned the 60's before. That was the great decade of Liberation. For the first time in the history of the world, mankind recognized that there were only two classes: the Oppressors and the Oppressed. All through history, you had class warfare: the rich against the poor, the noble against the peasant, the powerful nation against the weak, or non-existent nation. Finally, mankind recognized that most of you were oppressed, and you had to be liberated from your oppressors.

"There was a great movement in South America called 'Coscientizacao'. It was founded by a Brazilian named 'Paolo Freire'. His thesis was that people are only oppressed because they allow themselves to be oppressed by their oppressors. All they had to do was to stop letting the oppressors hold them down. This process he called 'conscienticization', which merely means 'coming to awareness' that you are letting yourself be oppressed. Once the masses come to the realization that they do not have to be oppressed, they will do whatever they have to do to end their oppression. In fact, once they realize that they are responsible for their own oppression, and stop allowing it to happen to them, the oppression is over. This is freedom and liberation. Nobody has to liberate them, because they have already liberated themselves by choosing freedom from oppression. (This, by the way, is what my wonderful American women have done over the past twenty years or so. They did not sit around begging to be liberated. They liberated themselves.

"Some great South American theologians developed a Theology of Liberation which was used as part of the conscienticization program, but it was condemned by the Church as nothing but warmed over 'Christian' Marxism.

"In most of South America there are only two classes: the rich and the poor. For our purposes you can call them the oppressors and the oppressed. For the most part, the Church hierarchy sided with the rich as it has always done since Columbus. So there you have it: the sordid story of freedom waiting to be born, both in South America and North America."

That was the longest lecture She ever gave me.

"Freedom waiting to be born in *North America*?" I quoted her. "But U.S.A is the 'Land of the free, and the home of the brave.' We are the first and best democracy in the world. We have fought all these wars to make the world safe for democracy.and freedom."

"No you haven't. You have sent the flower of your youth to die by the thousands to make the world safe for American capitalists!

"Why you are not even a democracy yourselves! You never have been. You were founded as an aristocracy, and you are more of an aristocracy today than you have ever been. Why there is only one member of congress who has a child in the Armed Forces! Ten percent of the people own ninety percent of the country. The other ninety percent have no idea they are oppressed, because they mistakenly think they can become a member of the aristocracy overnight if they get their kid into the right school, or manage to hit the lottery! You have no freedom at all, because the upper class is even more a slave to its wealth than the oppressed are!"

Did I detect a modicum of pique in her long rant against the U.S.A.?

"In the next session," I asked Her, "can we talk about freedom, and why I am not free?"

MY TENTH THERAPY SESSION WITH GOD

I was somewhat irritated that my therapist had used up my session on a tirade against the U.S.A. She sounded like Dorothy Day, The Berrigan brothers, and Charley Sheen, with a little Osama Bin Laden hot sauce thrown in for good measure.

I still didn't have a clue as to what freedom is. "A few sessions ago, you told me that I would know if I had grasped the truth about myself if I were free. But when I asked you how I would know if I'm free, you went on a long tirade about oppression, liberation, aristocracy, and capitalism. Now will you tell me what it means for *ME* to be free?"

"It means that you are not afraid to die. It means that you understand that the world belongs to you already and you belong to the world. When you own the whole world, you cannot lose it. You are free to let it go. Fear not, it will come back to you."

"But if I am dead," I begged Her, "how can the world come back to me?"

"When you are dead, *you* have gone back to the *world*."

"I want to understand what you are saying. It sounds so good, intellectually, in my head, but emotionally, in my gut, it scares me. Dead means to not be alive, and that hurts somebody who is alive like me."

"It doesn't hurt somebody who is dead like *Me*," God said.

"Can you properly be said to be dead?" I replied.

"Can you properly be said to be alive?" God asked.

"Wow! This is heavy", I said. "When I am alive, I'm not really alive, and when I am dead, I am not really dead?"

"Until you understand that there is no difference between life and death, you will never be free."

"There is no difference between life and death?" I repeated. "But isn't that what Buddhism has been teaching for centuries ?"

"You got it! They call it 'nirvana: the final freeing of the soul from all that enslaves it. Through enlightenment, one gives up all passions, all hatreds, all delusions and slips into the primordial sea of the womb, with no self-conscious ego, with no desires, and no fears."

"Talk about going home! You are saying that it's all about going back into the womb? But the fetus is not free. The fetus is trapped in solitary confinement like a prisoner."

"The fetus is free, because it is unborn and open to all possibilities: whether life or death or just existence. The fetus is free because it has an illusion of omnipotence." "I couldn't resist the temptation to say, "Do You have illusions of omnipotence?"

"No," She said, "I have neither illusions nor delusions of omnipotence. But very realistically, I wait like the fetus to be born in each and every human being."

I didn't even want to understand that. "I don't think this is helping my therapy. You seem to have your own problem about being born again in each of us. I thought each of *US* is supposed to be born again, not God."

"But didn't Francis of Assisi say 'It is in dying that we are born to eternal life'?"

"This is getting too scary for me", I said," Do you mind if we quit now, before I completely lose track of *what* I am. Forget about *who* I am!"

MY ELEVENTH THERAPY SESSION WITH GOD

This has happened to me in treatment before. I really began to lose my grip on myself. All this emphasis on nirvana and losing my ego, was beginning to shatter what meager grip I had on my inflated ego.

I spent the week in between sessions reviewing the ego-status of the main personality disorders I had dealt with in my career. I knew that the Narcissist has an infinitesimally small ego which the self- absorbed are constantly searching for, and which is so minute, that when they find it, they don't even recognize it. Then there was the poor borderline with an ego so shattered, it falls apart the more the borderline tries to grab on to it. Then there is the neurotic, with ego battered by its scrupulous super-ego, going through life from guilty bottom, and up over the hill to the next guilty bottom. Finally there goes the psychotic: a misbegotten body with a misdeveloped mind, coupled with an Id out of control, searching for an absent ego to guide it.

I know I'm not a narcissist or a borderline, because I have a swollen ego, grandiose in its own pomposity. I know I am not a psychotic, because psychotics do not have any ego to speak of. I guess I revert to being a neurotic of the histrionic or hysterical type, with a touch of manic exuberance. But for the past several years I have prided myself in doing my "Ego Integrity vs Despair" work, *a la* Erik Erikson. I thought I was finally getting my last task in psychosocial development completely under control. I thought I knew who I was, uniquely, as opposed to everyone else. I thought I had strung my life-events and decisions together into an acceptable Ego Integrity. Now God seemed to be telling me that I'm going to lose my ego entirely when I die. Not only that, but my ego has to die before my body does.

I dreaded facing the loss of my precious and pampered ego as I began my therapy session. "Isn't that what you have been trying to tell me? That I will no longer be afraid of death, because my ego will already be dead? That the only way I will not be afraid of dying is if I am convinced that death is better than life. And it is better than life because when we are dead, our ego is dead, and therefore no longer afraid of losing itself. So you are saying that the final task of life is to lose our ego, to die to our unique self?"

"Yes," God said, "Right now, you are in denial. I said before that all humans live in constant denial of death, and they cannot live in peace until they finally accept death as destiny, fulfillment, and peace. That's the shalom, the salaam, the peace you have been wished and wish others all your life."

"But," I complained, "accepting physical death is nothing compared to accepting spiritual death. 'What does it profit one if one gains the whole world, and loses oneself?' as Jesus said.

"Now you are saying what does it profit me if I gain myself, and then refuse to let my ego die? I have given a lifetime to establish the uniqueness of this one and only ego that I am, and now I have to throw it away?"

God lapsed into poetry. "Every human is like a snowflake: an incredibly beautiful, and unique, one of a kind, crystal. It has its brief moment of glory as it flies through the sky, and lands on earth. Some have a very short lifespan, some live for quite a long time, but eventually, they all melt into drops and join the vast blue ocean. Their unique identity is lost forever.

"Take your mother and father. They were two really unique human beings. They were born in Mineo, an ancient Greek city on top of a mountain 30 miles from Aetna, the highest mountain in Sicily. You know full well how special and unique they were. Now they are dead, but somehow alive in your heart. Remember 'Erin', your beautiful little Shi Tzu. She is dead, but lives on in your heart. So you will live on in My heart, and all that you love will live on in Me with you."

"But can't I have a stone with my name on it? Can't I have a book with my name on it?"

"None of this matters. We are talking about eternity, forever, here."

I tried to avoid the intensity of what She was saying. "When I was in the seminary in the 1950's there was a big to do about the Pope's infallibly declaring Mary's Assumption into heaven. I remember that we had a big conference to discuss not only Mary's bodily assumption into heaven, but her being saved from the ignominy of death. If Mary never died, what happened to her Ego?"

"You know you are only bringing this up to be facetious. You know there is no way the physical body of Jesus and Mary are out there in space wending their way through your local galaxy at the speed of light, heading for the neighboring galaxy. But as for Mary losing her ego, all humans must lose their ego. Why I'm God, and I don't even have an ego!"

And with that very unprofessional outburst, She ended the session.

My Twelfth Therapy Session with God

This therapy thing with God was getting out of hand. I had just finished telling Her that narcissists and borderlines have almost non-existent egos, and now She was telling me She had no ego at all? Was God the divine narcissist or the eternal borderline, futilely searching for an ego?

She knew exactly what I was thinking, but like a professional therapist, she let me begin the session.

"Why are you looking for an ego?" I asked.

"You dummy, who said I was looking for an ego? And besides, don't try to psych me out, this is *your* therapy. You tried doing therapy on *Me*, and you botched it all up. I should sue you for malpractice!"

"Don't try that in an American court. It's against the Constitutional Amendment about the separation of church and state. And besides, I dare you to find a lawyer or an insurance company that believes in God."

"Touche`," She said. "You are not so dumb as to think this little diversion is going to get you off the hook for calling me a narcissist or a borderline?"

"I never said that- I only thought it!" "Nice try!" God said. "To answer your question, I am not a narcissist or a borderline, or any diagnosis in Ego Psychology, because I don't have any ego at all. You have to be self-conscious to have an ego, and you have told me a thousand times that I am unconscious being."

"But a rock is an unconscious being!" "Dummy, a rock is *AN* unconscious being. I *AM* unconscious being itself."

"But if you are the Ground of All Being, why aren't you the Ground of Conscious Being?"

God would not let me off the hook. "Again, that is a very intellectual, philosophical question. Save it for your next book. Right now, stick with your intuition. You sense, intuitively, that God is unconscious. You went through all of that in your first couple of sessions above. You sense that God is a metaphor or symbol that you self-conscious beings use to talk about the Source of All Being and Existence. The only verifiable conscious expression of reality going on right now is in you self-conscious beings. At this stage in the development of consciousness, you are coming to see that the Source of All Being created, evolved, emanated, whatever word you want to use. So you are the lucky result of that emanation."

She went on, "To put it in other terms, the Source of All Being, gave off sparks of consciousness, and those sparks gave off further sparks of self-consciousness."

I struggled to follow Her. "So the first sparks of consciousness were some kind of sentient life that evolved into self-conscious beings like me?"

"Yes, but don't be so philosophical about it, because the philosophers and scientists will clobber you. Stay with your intuition"

I struggled still to understand. "So, intuitively, I perceive the Source of Being, emanating into a self-conscious being, who becomes the spokesman for the unconscious Ground of Being which cannot express itself directly, but only indirectly through me."

"Yes, except you must use spokesperson, or the ladies reading this will be very mad at you."

"Yes, yes. So all of this is your way of saying that you have no ego, basically, and all of us must be the little egos for the big ego in the sky?"

"Now I know you are putting me on," God said, exasperated with me. "Actually, ego was invented by Freud as part of his topographical explanation of the psyche. He said that the latter consisted of Ego- Superego- and Id. But remember these are only symbolic or metaphorical terms, just as the very term for God is. Just, in fact, as most human Bibles and Scriptures are."

"But aren't the Scriptures all 'revealed' by God?"

"Again, you gotta be kidding. How can I 'reveal' anything, since I am not even conscious, let alone, *self*-conscious. This is all stuff that people like you dreamed up from their unconscious intuition and 'revealed' to us in the name of God. Most of them probably thought that God was dictating all that stuff to them."

"The great 'Dictator in the Sky', I quipped. "Sounds like Mussolini."

"No, it sounds like *you*."

MY THIRTEENTH THERAPY SESSION WITH GOD

I was delighted at the wonderful sense of humor that my Divine Therapist had. Of course, throughout the ages God always was a real laugher, but this aspect of God was lost on most uptight believers. Even Jesus, as grim and somber as his life was depicted by the 'Sacred' writers, must have had to excuse himself many times and gone off into the woods and have a real belly laugh for himself at the antics of his followers. Which brings us to my thirteenth therapy session with the 'Great Laugher in the Sky'"

"I heard you", said my therapist. "You enjoy nothing more than laughing at Me."

"I'm not laughing AT you, I'm laughing WITH you."

"No, it's more like you are laughing FOR me. Did you ever think that the most noble, exalted pursuit of a human being is to be God's official voice of laughter? If that doesn't inflate your ego, nothing will."

"Can we get back to Freud and the human ego?"

"Actually," She began, "Jung's idea of the *self* is better than Freud's idea of the ego. For Jung, the self, with a small 's' is the center of consciousness and self- consciousness in the individual. For Jung, Self with a capital 'S' was the symbol for God. God was not exactly the collective unconscious, but He was like the ocean of unconscious being, and each little 'self' was a drop in that ocean of unconsciousness, and you each rise to the surface to become a pinpoint of consciousness in the unconscious ocean."

"I guess Jung was trying to say that God was the great unconscious Self of the universe, and we each are the small self- conscious selves of the universe?"

"Yes, and as I said before, each of you is like that unique little crystal of snow, transparent in the sun, shining brightly in your glory, before you melt into the ocean. Better still you are like the May fly which comes out of its cocoon and is born to live for just one day. It copulates, reproduces and then dies during its one and only day in the sun. Except that for you, your one day in the sun is forever."

"How can it be forever?"

"It is forever, not just because the poet says, 'A thing of beauty is a joy forever'. It is so because in dying you pass from the dimension of time into the dimension of eternity."

"But if I can't take my ego or my self with me, why would I want to go?"

"Because you have no choice."

"But Jesus said, 'What does it profit a man if he gains the whole world, and loses himself?'"

"You still don't get it, do you? You have always understood Jesus as talking about your ego, your self, and how you will gain yourself if you lose yourself. Now you have to take Jesus one step further and accept that you must lose your self, period."

"Is that what they mean by the 'leap of faith'?"

"I don't know what 'they' mean, but I mean that you must be like a little girl on the second floor of a burning house. She hears her father on the ground outside her window, crying to her to throw herself out the window, and he will catch her. You must have the courage of that little girl and jump out into the darkness of death, with only your faith in the eternal source of being that somehow you will not be lost, but found."

"So that is what I have to do when I die? A leap of faith?"

"No, you have to do it *now*, before you die."

"You mean, I have to follow Your voice, and throw my ego and my self out the window into the darkness outside?"

"That's right!"

"And what shall I say to the psychiatrist who examines me in the psych emergency ward?"

"Are you trying to make a joke out of the most serious thing I have ever told you? Do you realize that this means you are in denial about the loss of self that I have been talking about for the last two months?"

She cut the session short so I could sweat about my denial of the loss of self until next week.

My Fourteenth Therapy Session with God

I knew, from the conclusion of the last session, that I was getting into the climax of my therapy. Completely unexpectedly my treatment had been turned topsy-turvy. I started my therapy looking for my identity, and now I was being challenged to voluntarily dispose of my identity. I was supposed to be a bright burning flame in the fire of God's eternal love, and now I was a fast disintegrating ember. Not only, but I was supposed to commit identity suicide and cast myself into the darkness.

I was afraid to ask my divine therapist if I had the suicide thing right. But, of course, She knew what I was thinking.

"I know it sounds preposterous to you. You have spent 74 years trying to build and defend an ego that would be impervious to death, and thus live forever. Now I am asking you to give up that ego."

"But isn't that what mental patients do when their mechanisms of defense of the ego collapse, and they have a nervous breakdown, and end up in a psychiatric 'institute'?"

"That is completely different," She said. "The poor mental patient has such meager grasp on a very tentative ego that it is very easy to lose it in a crisis. In your case, you have a reasonably secure hold on your unique ego. Now you must have faith, and let your ego die a natural death."

"But egos take so long to build, they don't die easily."

"That's why you have to help them along by jumping into the darkness outside."

"But that's suicide!"

"Not if it's your own ego, and you are finally free to let it go!"

"You know what this sounds like? It sounds like those crazy Muslim Jihad suicide bombers!"

"No, it sounds like God. Your fellow ex- priest, Jack Miles, wrote a book called, *Christ: A Crisis in the Life of God.* In it Miles revives the ancient Christian theology of the first centuries about the suicide of Christ. The early theologians took Jesus' words literally: 'No one is taking (my life) from me. I lay it down of my own accord.'"

"Miles implies that Jesus Christ, as God, chose to die. Now I am saying that was the beginning of the death of theism. God, the Father of Jesus, was the old Hebrew God, promoted from a tribal god to the universal God of Monotheism. He becomes human in Christ, and kills himself. His ego as a separate unique person was supposed to die in Jesus, but the Greeks and Romans resurrected Jesus as the Ego God, and invented the elaborate theology of the Trinity. Not content with one big Ego for God, they gave God three Egos. They came perilously close to giving God a multiple personality disorder. But instead they carried the idea of God as a separate divine Person, or rather Three Divine Persons, right into the Twenty First Century.

"Now, hopefully, the multiple suicide attacks of 9/11/01 have brought attention to the fact that this personal God of monotheism is a dying old man indeed."

I couldn't wait to break in to this dreadfully long monologue. I know my patients hate it when I intellectualize so long. But I had the presence of mind to realize that my divine therapist was coming to the most important part of my therapy.

"Are you saying that just as Jesus died to his ego by committing suicide, so do I have to die to my ego by committing suicide?"

"I thought you would never get it!"

My Fifteenth Therapy Session with God

This was a very bad week for me. God had said that I got it, but I didn't. Ego suicide was a new concept for me. The suicide of God was hard enough to take, but the suicide of my ego was another story. God's suicide was *His* problem, after all, and He was God, and better equipped to solve such problems than I am. Nothing that I had ever studied or read, or experienced, prepared me for the suicidal death of my own ego. I know the Buddhists, when they talk about *nirvana*, mean that the human person must sink into the ocean of unconsciousness. But as far as I know, they are not burdened with the Western idea of the ego. So it was up to my divine therapist to enlighten me.

"Help, I'm stuck", I asked Her.

"If I had an ego, I would say, 'I know', but absent an ego, I can only say with President Clinton, 'Ah feel yo' pain'."

"This was the closest to a prayer I felt for a long, long time. Please God, I need you now! I'm terrified, and I haven't got a clue what to do!"

"Typical you- you always want to *do* something. You don't have to *do* anything. I've told you a million times, 'Don't just *do* something, *stand there!*'"

"You are right, as usual. If I am sure of my ego I don't have to hold on to it any more, I don't have to cling to it. I can let it go. I remember being so impressed with my classmate Gino McAlee's description of the first appearance of the Risen Christ. It was to Mary Magdalen, and she ran and knelt down and grabbed on to Jesus's legs. Jesus said, 'Don't try to hang on to me. You don't have to cling to me anymore. I am with you always, even to the end of time.'"

"Exactly," God said. "You don't have to hold on to me, because I am part of you, and you are part of Me. In fact, we have become One."

"Is that what all that theology about the mystical body of Christ was all about? We have become Christ in our world today?"

"That's right. God has no ego, Christ has no ego, you have no ego. We are all One and there is no argument about who is who."

"You mean all that emphasis on acquiring an ego was just a construct we used to learn how to be mature human beings? Sort of a 'training ego'?"

"It is an idea that seems to work for people brought up in the western psychological tradition. It's a fine idea, but has to be understood correctly. My children of the East don't seem to need an ego. Perhaps there are so many of them that egos grated on each other."

"Are you implying that because they never developed a psychology of the ego, that they never developed a theology of a Supreme Being with an ego?"

God really trumped me on this play. "No, it was the other way around. Because they never experienced Me as an ego, they never experienced themselves as egos."

"Wow!" I was astonished. "You are blaming theism, read: the idea of a God with an ego, on Abraham and the Jews?"

"I said nothing of the kind. The Hebrews were, indeed, ahead of everyone else in God-consciousness. They were the first ones to take their tribal god and name Him Universal God of all tribes. They thus made Him into a person who intervened directly in history for their tribe. Only later did the idea of 'person' evolve into the idea of 'ego'. But I remained my good old unselfconscious Self."

"You sound like Ronald Reagan with Alzheimer's, not knowing he was President."

"But Regan didn't know he was president *while* he was president! It was just the best acting gig of his life."

"When you came to me for therapy, you said that the God of Monotheism, the old guy with the beard whom Michelangelo painted on the ceiling of the Sistine Chapel, had Alzheimer's."

"I was only kidding. But I do want to say Jack Miles got it right in his book about the suicide of God, only he didn't go far enough. The God of the Bible, that is, the God of Theism, killed himself in the person of Jesus Christ, in order to do away forever with the idea that God is a self-conscious person. The only problem is it is taking two thousand years for the three big Monotheistic religions to get this message."

Maybe the disgrace of the fundamentalists in this terrorism-antiterrorism thing will finally send the old 'guy in the sky' to his well-deserved grave."

"You really enjoy knocking the 'old guy in the sky'", I said.

"Even though I don't have an ego I can still have fun!"

"How I wish the fundamentalists could see the humor in it, too! But they are so afraid of losing the 'old man in the sky' God. He did a lot of good things. He took care of evil by punishing evil doers with threat of hell."

God laughed at that one. "Yeah, sure, hell prevented about as many crimes as the death penalty prevents."

"But heaven was such a great idea! It sustained millions of poor suffering souls throughout the ages".

"But Karl Marx was right. Heaven was used by the rich as the opium of the people, so they didn't have to share their wealth with the poor. 'Let them wait for heaven'"

"But I adored the old man in the sky. He was a real Santa Claus. He came through for me, time and time again."

"That was Me, the Ground of All Being, who came through for you!"

"But I needed Someone whom I could picture, Someone I could feel, Someone I could experience, Someone I could talk to!"

"But you are doing it right now, and I am not some divine person, nor the Big Ego in the Sky.

"Sorry, your time is up," She said and softly slipped out of consciousness.

My Sixteenth Therapy Session with God

All I could think of during the week was how much I missed the old God I had grown up with, and how I was still mourning the loss of my ego, even though I had not lost it yet. As for the former, I began to mourn the old grandpa in the sky.

I had never realized how much I had projected my own grandfather on to God. He was my mother's father. (My paternal grandfather had died in Sicily over a hundred years ago.) But my maternal grandfather, after whom I was named, never spoke a word of English, even though he was in the U.SA. for over fifty years. I, of course, never spoke a word of Sicilian, his only language. Even when I finally learned Italian in school, we couldn't converse, because he didn't know Italian. So, obviously, I must have made God my grandpa. Once I got over the Last Judgment with God the grandfather, and the eternal flames of Hell, I developed a great relationship with God. Finally, a grandfather I could talk to! He was a delight to be with.

When I began my Sixteenth therapy session with God, I told him about my grandfather God and how much I missed him since He died.

God was not that impressed. "God the Almighty Grandfather in Heaven was way too human for my taste. True, Jesus called me 'Abba' or 'Daddy' in Aramaic, and for two thousand years, this metaphor helped millions of people find the divine in their human hearts. At least it was better than Yahweh, Jehova, or Adonai, as the Hewbrews called me, or Allah as the Muslims did. These terms were not human, so they were really aloof. They kept people from cuddling up to me."

"That's what I mean. You were a cuddly God for me. Now I can't warm up to You as the 'Ground of All Being'"

"But don't you see that I am even closer to you than a Teddy Bear! I am closer to you than you are to your own self! Don't you see that you and I are One?"

I kept repeating to myself, like Jesus, "'The Father and I are one', and 'All I have is yours, Father, and all you have is mine.'"

"And you are God's and God is yours", She said, over and over, as in a lullaby. "Not like a grandpa's lullaby, but your own inner peace humming to you."

"I feel better now. We can go and bury Grandpa God, but what about my ego? I am not ready to bury *that* yet. When I was in high school and read Edgar Allen Poe, I was terrified of being buried alive! Now I have that same fear of dying and finding my ego buried alive".

"I am going to teach you how to let your ego go, right now before your body dies. Do you remember how you learned to treat people who were suffering from hypochondria? Remember they had real pain and suffering, and it came mostly from the fear that they were dying? You can't cure the hypochondriac, but you can teach him how to live with his pain. You have to convince him that if he dies he will no longer suffer the pain of dying, because he will be dead. So, if he really thinks about it, death will suddenly become good because it will be the end of his pain and suffering. Then all of a sudden, he is no longer afraid of dying, and the fear of dying becomes acceptable and normal.

"You must do the same. Right now, the fear of losing your ego is paralyzing. You have spent 74 years building and defending that Ego. Now, for the last ten years, you have been following Erik Erikson's last task of life, namely: Ego Integrity vs Despair. You were mislead by Erikson to think that despair comes from failure to integrate your ego, that is, make it whole and in sync with your entire life's journey. Erikson was wrong. Despair comes from desperately trying to cling to an ego that will be nothing but excess baggage when you die."

"It's funny that you should say that about Erik Erikson. A couple of years ago, my friend, Andy Costello, sent me an article from Atlantic Monthly by Erikson's daughter. In it, she said that her father actually died in despair, because he had been convinced all his life that he was the illegitimate child of the King of Denmark, and had never been acknowledged as of royal lineage. Thus his ego was tormented in the end because he never was given the recognition that he deserved. Poor Erikson succumbed, like so many of the Freudians, to the cult of the ego. Why Freud, himself, actually thought that he was the Messiah. This cult of the ego has led to the shameful worship of celebrity in western society. You now have movie stars, rock stars, athletes, politicians, who become so famous and celebrated that they become household words. Remember the Beatles bragging in the sixties that they had become more popular than Jesus Christ?"

God responded, "Failed Presidents, like Johnson, Nixon, Bush number one, and Clinton, were only worried about their 'legacy', not about inspiring or leading your poor country. Let them take solace in death looking at all the greenbacks with their pictures on them.

"And, of course, you think you are going to become famous by writing these silly little books."

"I definitely am not going to become famous from writing these books. I'll be lucky if I can coax or cajole a hundred of my relatives, friends and acquaintances to read them. Why, I can't even get my wife to read them!

"But maybe you are right about my secretly hoping for fame. I remember when my mother was dying, back in 1967. We were in her hospital room with my sister and my niece. My sister was combing my mother's hair, and my mother said to my niece, 'Watch what your mother is doing, because some day you are going to be combing *her* hair. And look at your uncle Sal. Someday he is going to be famous.'

"It's funny how that prediction of a dying mother has stayed with me."

God became very motherly, "Every dying mother thinks her son is going to become famous some day. It's part of her own wish for immortality. Somehow, through her son, she would live on. But she doesn't need you. She lives forever in Me, and so will you. And both your ego's will be jumbled in the stars. Remember the child, Therese of Lisieux, who was walking and holding her father's hand, and looked up at the sword of Orion, at the big letter 't' and said, 'Look,Daddy, God has written my name in the sky!' No, I didn't. All your names in the stars will be jumbled, and you will be written on my heart, with no name. Have you heard the advertisements lately asking for money to name a star after yourself or after one of your loved ones? All the stars have everyone's name on them, but they will remain WITHOUT name forever.

"It is time for you to go."

My Seventeenth Therapy Session with God

I sensed that God was through with my therapy, and was trying to ease my separation-anxiety which occurs at the end of every course of treatment.

"I need you," I said, "To help me say goodbye to my ego." And I became more than somewhat weepy.

"You know, I poured a lot of pain and suffering into this ego. It suffered guilt, loss, terror, and depression."

"Then you should be glad to get rid of it!"

"But I invested so much time and energy into my ego, so much anxiety and sleepless nights. So many 'Examinations of Conscience', kept so many rules and regulations. Even though I broke many, I kept even more. I worked so hard to get people to accept me, to like me, even, God forbid, love me. All for the exaltation of my miserable fucking ego!" I began very softly, I might say *pianissimo*, then gradually went through *piano*, until I reached *forte* and then *fortissimo,* and when I shouted the "f" word, I was in full *crescendo.*

"You know you only use that word when you are angry," God said. "What are you so mad about?"

"All the wasted years! My life was a fucking ego trip! It benefited absolutely no one, especially my self!"

God was not that sympathetic. "You have never been able to separate well. Every time you have to say goodbye to someone, you always manage to say something stupid, something hurtful, so they will be glad to let you go, and you won't miss them. You have had some truly miserable break-ups."

"But this time, it being the last time I get to see my ego, I really am sorry to let it go."

"Of course you are. So why do your usual 'I hate you, I never liked you routine?' Why pretend that your life was a stupid waste, so you can let it go easier?

"Remember Kuhbler Ross's second stage of death is anger, and you are deep into it right now."

My hurt was too great to really say it. "I am very lazy, and I can't bear to think that I worked so much harder than I needed to. Maybe there is something I can salvage from my ego trip. I am such a pack rat, there must be something I can keep, out a lifetime of ego work!"

"Let it all go, and get into your depression and loss funk."

"It feels so much like losing my self. How can I let go of myself? Remember that play, *A Thousand Clowns*? It was about identity. The uncle who had custody of his nephew wanted him to know why he was born a man and not a chair! I worked my ass off all my life, to find out who I was as opposed to everyone else. And now you are asking me to throw my unique identity into the garbage. You want me to become one other brick in a building full of billions of bricks?"

"That's right. I want you all to be identical. I made you all unique. It was your job to become identical."

"Now that is really depressing!"

"Ah feel yo' pain!" she did her Bill Clinton again. "I had to give up my ego a long time ago. In fact, I never had an ego. I was content to let all of you name me.

And most of you did a terrible job of identifying Me.

"I don't care at all for the Judeo- Christian Bible's description of Me. You make me too distant, too awesome, too judgmental, too punishing. And the Muslim idea of Me as Allah is very unappealing, aloof, even embarrassing. At least the rest of the religions leave me alone, ignore me, or just worship their ancestors instead of me."

I could tell that God was depressed at the terrible image the Monotheists of the world had projected on Her throughout the centuries. So I repeated to her the paean I had given her at the end of her therapy sessions with me:

"You are the joy of making love, the bubble of a baby's smile.

"You are the tear in the toddler's eye, the prettiness of the puppy.

"You are the silence of the slave, weeping to be freed, the gall of the oppressed struggling to survive.

"You are the compassion for the poor, the strength of the meek.

"You are the hope of those who wait, the security of those who believe.

"You are the freedom of the prisoner, the forgiveness of the condemned.

"You are the loveliness of the leaf, the green in the billowing grass.

"You are the fragrance of the flower, the shelter of the trees.

"You are the broadness of the plains, the snow-covered awe of mountains.

"You are the blue sky, and sun-filled clouds.

"You are the aquamarine waters of the ocean, the sweep of the continents.

"You are the Holder of the Globe, hurler of the Moon, the infinite power of suns, and the breathtaking awe of planets and their satellites.

"You are the gravity of the galaxies, the force of the universe, the Strider of the Milky Way, the Fourth of July explosions of nebulae. You are the One, the True, the Good, and the Beautiful. You are the Ground of All Being. You are Ultimate Concern.

"You are Love."

While I was singing her praises, she looked at me with a quizzical, unseeing look, and I knew for the first time in my life what the medieval mystic meant when he called God *The Cloud of Unknowing.* Here was somebody who was really a nobody, and had no way of being impressed with her own magnificence and beauty.

She knew exactly what I was thinking, and She said to me, "Sing that same song to yourself, because it is equally true of you, and keep singing it until you are no longer impressed by your own magnificence, until, in fact, you become one with your magnificence. And then go out into the universe and sing that song to every creature, until they are no longer impressed with their own magnificence.

"And then God will be All in All."

"And then God will be All in All," I said, over and over again, until She disappeared into the Cloud of Unknowing.

An Evaluation of God as Therapist

G OD DID AN excellent job as a therapist for me, considering She
was just an amateur. Like all beginning therapists, she talked
much more than she needed to. At least She had plenty to say
that was right to the point. She was totally devoid of the self-absorbed
'yada-yada yada' of the Seinfeld sitcom sillies, which I have to say is not
true of most therapists these days. (Now it can be told! Why just look
at me!)

But I do have to say that She often injected her own problems into
my therapy! God knows that I do it all the time, but I was expecting a
little more class from Her. (I know I am getting away with absolutely
nothing with this critique. She will be waiting to get her divine hands
on me.) To the point, She missed the pain I had in putting to death my
own precious ego. How can I blame her, since She is Unconscious Being,
and therefore never had so much as a breath of an ego?

But I do thank God for guiding me straight down the fall line of my
own gravity, into the depths of my emptiness.

Only someone who had never had an ego could have led me into
the dark night of the ego. Four hundred and fifty years ago, St. John of
the Cross had suffered through the dark night of the senses, and the
dark night of the soul. But the dark night of the ego goes beyond both.
I now realize that John's dark night of the senses was depression, or as
the Greeks called it *anhedonia, 'an inability to experience pleasure'*. Then
John continued through the darkness into the night of the soul. I now
realize that the night of the soul was a loss of spiritual joy and exaltation.

But now that I have gone through the dark night of the ego, I can say that the darkness goes beyond pleasure, beyond joy, to a loss of the sense of being my own person. But worst of all is the sense of emptiness and loss at the death of a personal God, and the death of my own ego.

As God said in the therapy, quoting Jesus, "What does it profit a man if he gains the whole world and then loses himself?" Now, after I had followed that large bit of wisdom all my life, God continues, "Now that you have given up the world in order to gain yourself, you must give up yourself, too. You must die to your own unique ego, which you were hoping would live forever. But hardest of all, you must give up the idea of a Father in Heaven who is there to answer your every prayer, as if it was Christmas every day.

CONCLUSION

From Thomas Merton

"**M**EDITATION AND NONVIOLENCE are directed toward the protection of life in oneself and in others, while at the same time uniting compassion and detachment, insight and pity.

"But is the Buddhist meditation on suffering, in order to attain deliverance from ignorance and 'round of birth and death,' not morbid, masochistic? Does it not instill a contempt for life itself? Suzuki says:

'The value of human life lies in the fact of suffering, for where there is no suffering, no consciousness of karmic bondage, there will be no power of attaining spiritual experience and thereby reaching the field of non-distinction. ***Unless we agree to suffer we cannot be free from suffering.***'" (Essence of Buddhism)

Zen and the Birds of Appetite, By Thomas Merton, New Directions, NY, 1968

Thomas Merton, in *Zen and the Birds of Appetite*[1] says that man has a mysterious tendency to falsify his relationship to the world. (Buddhists call this *Avidya* or "ignorance.")

Merton goes on to say, "It (avidya) is a disposition to treat the ego as an absolute and central reality and to refer all things to it as objects of desire or of repulsion. Christianity attributes this view of man and

---

[1] Thomas Merton, *Zen and the Birds of Appetite*, New York, New Directions,1968, pps.82,83,&84

of reality to 'original sin'....The story of the Fall tells us in mythical language that 'original sin' is not simply a stigma arbitrarily making good pleasures seem guilty, but a basic inauthenticity....It implies a determined willfulness in trying to make things be other than they are in order that we may be able to make them subserve, at any moment, to our individual desire for pleasure or for power.

"As long as this 'brokenness' of existence continues, there is no way out of the inner contradictions that it imposes upon us....If desire itself is a kind of fracture, every movement of desire is a movement, and therefore causes pain. The desire to remain immobile is a movement. The desire to escape is a movement. The desire for *nirvana* is a movement. The desire for extinction is a movement. Yet there is no way for us to be still by 'imposing stillness' on the desires. In a word, desire cannot stop itself from desiring, and it must continue to move and hence to cause pain even when it seeks liberation from itself and desires its own extinction.

"The Buddhist answer is in the four noble truths by which, following the teaching and experience of Buddha, man seeks to apprehend the real nature of his existence and to patiently rediscover his real roots in the true ground of all being. When man is grounded in authentic truth and love the roots of desire themselves wither, brokenness is at en end, and truth is found in the wholeness and simplicity of *nirvana*: perfect awareness and perfect compassion. *Nirvana* is the wisdom of perfect love grounded in itself and shining through everything, meeting with no opposition. The heart of brokenness is then seen for what it was: an illusion, but persistent and invincible illusion of the isolated ego-self, setting itself up in opposition to love, demanding that its own desire be accepted as the law of the universe, and hence suffering from the fact that by its desire it is fractured in itself and cut off from the loving wisdom in which it should be grounded.

"Buddhism refuses to countenance any self- cultivation of the soul. It ruthlessly exposes any desire of enlightenment or of salvation that seeks merely the glorification of the ego and the satisfaction of its desires in a transcendent realm. It is not that this is 'wrong' or 'immoral' but that it is simply impossible. Ego-desire can never culminate in happiness, fulfillment and peace, because it is a fracture which cuts us off from the ground of reality in which truth and peace are found. As long as the ego seeks to 'grasp' or 'contain' that ground as an objective content of awareness, it will be frustrated and broken….

"For selfish desire there is and can be no fulfillment and no salvation. The only salvation, as Christ said, is found in losing oneself- that is by opening oneself to the other as another self….

"As the Buddhists say, *nirvana* is found in the midst of the world around us, and the truth is not *somewhere else.*"

I was very pleased to find Thomas Merton's explanation of Zen Buddhism and Nirvana on my bookshelf, where it lay untouched for almost thirty years. I needed this kind of corroboration of my theory on the death of the ego. However, I feel that I have gone beyond Buddhism in so far as I have related the death of the individual go to the death of God as we have hitherto known Him, that is, as a theistic projection.

As I have tried to explain many times, God as a projection of theism means that for the past three thousand years, human beings have created God in their own image and likeness. How were they to know otherwise? Since humans, especially in the western world, were naturally prone to self-will and ego, self-consciousness and self-aggrandizement, they imagined that God would have these qualities, too, to an infinite degree. As tribes merged into nations and empires, people needed to project these qualities of power, knowledge, and authority on to their kings and emperors. And naturally, as the divine rights of kings began to grow, the divine rights of God grew even greater. We could no sooner imagine a God who would be selfless as a king who would be so.

A remarkable Jewish-American scholar, Richard Rubenstein, wrote *When Jesus Became God*[2], a splendid description of the political process in which the humble Jew, Jesus, was drafted by the Roman Emperor to be the God of Christianity. It was simply unthinkable for the head of a religion to be anything but an omnipotent God. Of course, Jesus

---

[2]   Rubenstein, Richard, *When Jesus Became God*, Harcourt, New York,1999

was divinized into a very theistic personal God, and the Trinity had to be 'invented' to make room for three persons in God, all of them omnipotent, and omniscient, even though they all shared in one divine 'nature.'

Around twenty five years ago, I had come to the conclusion that the God I had grown up with never existed in reality. Most people in our culture have an experience similar to mine when they realize that Santa Claus never existed. But the experience of losing the Divine Santa Claus is infinitely more traumatizing than that of losing the Christmas Santa Claus, because it occurs at a much later age and without any substitute experiences that take the place of the lost Santa Claus. For me, it caused a mid-life crisis, because I was living the lifestyle of a dedicated religious priest that was totally dependent on the existence of a theistic God.

Yet many of my colleagues remained at their posts, either by refusing to accept the change in the idea of God, or by adapting the new idea of God to the old lifestyle. Many, indeed, left the priesthood, but held on to the theistic idea of God. It is for each of us to look again within ourselves and find a concept of God that we can live with.

I will share with you a paper I wrote while undergoing my own mid-life crisis. It was on existential neurosis. I had discovered the existential theologian, Paul Tillich, who wrote *The Courage To Be*. In it, Tillich talks about the process of disillusionment that religious people go through when they have to give up their childish fantasies of a 'cosmic Papa', who is going to take care of us, and, of course, give meaning to our lives by rewarding good and punishing evil. According to my paper, we had to come to the realization that we had been using religion as a neurotic way of avoiding loneliness and anxiety and, of course, dealing with death. Tillich says, "It is as atheistic to affirm the existence of God as it is to deny it. God is being itself, not *A* being." Tillich goes on to say that one must give up the God of theism in order to be grasped by the "God above the God of theism." In other words, Tillich affirms that the "courage to be" results from experiencing oneself as "being grasped by the power of Being itself." Very subtly, the existential therapist helps his client to see that accepting the anxiety of non-being is a great courageous act of commitment to whatever being there is in our ability to accept the unacceptable: the meaninglessness of our lives ! For many, this goes beyond words to explain. It is an intuitive insight that one can indeed accept acceptance by the transcendent power of Being that gives meaning to life.

In place of what we used to call "faith", we now need "commitment" to existence, as the existentialists call it. We "create", as it were, our own existence, by making a conscious commitment to existence. We use our human will and intellect to grab on to our own being and existence.

Dag Hammarskjold, the deceased Secretary General of the United Nations, has become a model of modern existential man and woman. He seems to have made this authentic commitment to self, mankind, and world. Shortly before he died he wrote in *Markings*: "I don't know Who or What- put the question, I don't know when it was put, I don't even remember answering, but at some moment I did answer *YES* to Someone or Something- and from that hour I was certain that existence is meaningful and therefore my life, in self- surrender, had a goal." [3]

All the elements are there for the ideal existentialist : an intuitive grasp of meaning, and commitment to a goal. But the paradox is even deeper when we read what Hammarskjold wrote just before his tragic death: "I came to a time and place where I realized that the Way leads to a triumph which is a catastrophe, and to a catastrophe which is a triumph, that the price for committing one's life would be reproach, and the only elevation possible to man lies in the depths of humiliation."

Now, after 25 years since I wrote those words, it is very poignant to me what a Christ figure Dag Hammarskjold has turned out to be. In his words of catastrophe becoming triumph, and elevation lying in humiliation, we see the crucifixion and then resurrection of Christ that has come to be the paradigm of existential commitment for the ages.

Little did I know that the horrific events of September 11 would be the watershed event that proved once and for all that the Ego God of theism was dead, and along with Him, my own ego was doomed to die.

---

[3]   Hammarskjold, Dag, *Markings*

The therapy I did with God was painful, but God never promised me a rose garden. The death of such an ego as mine could not be a pretty one. But that pain produced an insight into world class ego: the ego of tribes and nations living for their own selfish sakes. Even more than individual ego, the ego of tribes and nations was threatening to destroy life on earth itself. My newfound commitment to existence led me to address the world and its own threatened existence.

Would the world submit to group therapy with me and my co-therapist, God, at the United Nations in New York?

That, of course, is the subject of my next book.

See you then.

Bibliography

Berry, Thomas. *The Dream of the Earth.* San Francisco: Sierra Club Books, 1998

The Book of Tao, Peter Pauper Press, Mt. Vernon, NY, 1962.

Crossan, Dominic, *The Birth of Christianity: Discovering What Happened in the Years Immediately after the Execution of Jesus,* HarperSanFrancisco, 1998

Becker, Ernest, *The Denial of Death*, Free Press Paperbacks, Simon & Schuster, NY 1997

Finley, James. *Merton's Palace of Nowhere: A Search for God through Awareness of the True Self.* Notre Dame, Ind. Ave Maria Press, 1978.

Fox, Matthew. *Original Blessing: A Primer in Creation Spirituality.* Santa Fe, NM, Bear & Company, 1983

Hammarskjold, Dag, *Markings*, tr. By Leif Sjoberg & W.H. Auden, NY, Knopf, 1964

May, Rollo, *Man's Search for Himself*, Dell Publishing, NY NY 1953.

May, Rollo, Ernest Angel, and Henri Ellenberger, Editors, *Existence,* Simon and Schuster,NY, NY,1958.

Merton, Thomas, *Zen and the Birds of Appetite*, New Directions,1968.

Miles, Jack. *God: A Biography.* New York. Random House, 1996.

Miles, Jack. *Christ: A Crisis in the Life of God.* New York. Alfred A Knopf.

Morwood, Michael. *Is Jesus God? Finding Our Faith* New York. Crossroads Books, 2001.

O'Murchu, Diarmuid, *Evolutionary Faith*, Orbis Books, 2002.

Otto, Rudolf. *Mysticism East and West.* New York. Macmillan, 1970.

Padovano, Anthony, *A Retreat with Thomas Merton*, Cincinnati, OH, St. Anthony Messenger Press, 1995.

Progoff, Ira. *The Cloud of Unknowing: A New Translation of the Medieval Classic on Mysticism*. New York. The Julian Press,1957.

Rubenstein, Richard. *When Jesus Became God: The Struggle to Define Christianity during the Last Days of Rome*. San Diego:Harcourt, 2000

Spong, John Shelby, *Here I, Stand* San Francisco, Harper, 1999.

Spong, John Shelby, *Liberating the Gospels: Freeing Jesus From 2000 years of Misunderstanding*, Harper, San Francisco, 1996.

Spong, John Shelby, *Why Christianity Must Change or Die: A Bishop Speaks to Believers in Exile*. San Francisco, HarperSanFrancisco, 1998

Spong John Shelby, *A New Christianity For A New World: Why Traditional Faith Is Dying And How A New Faith Is Being Born*. San Francisco, Harper, 2001.

Teilhard DeChardin, Pierre, *Christianity and Evolution*. NewYork:Harcourt Brace Jovanovich, 1971

Teilhard DeChardin, Pierre, *The Divine Milieu:An Essay on the Interior Life*. New York: Harper and Row, 1968

Teilhard DeChardin, Pierre, *Human Energy*. New York: Harcourt Brace Jovanovich, 1971:

Teilhard DeChardin, Pierre, *The Phenomenon of Man*, New York: Harper and Row, 1961

Tillich, Paul, *The Courage To Be*, New Haven, Yale Press, 1953

Willis,Robert, Ph.D. *Transcendence in Relationship: Existentialism and Psychotherapy*, Ablex Pubishing Corp., Norwood, NJ, 1994

BACK TO EARTH

Back To Earth
Life and Death Without Ego

A Spirituality For the Age of Terrorism/ From Humus To Human and Back

By Sal Umana

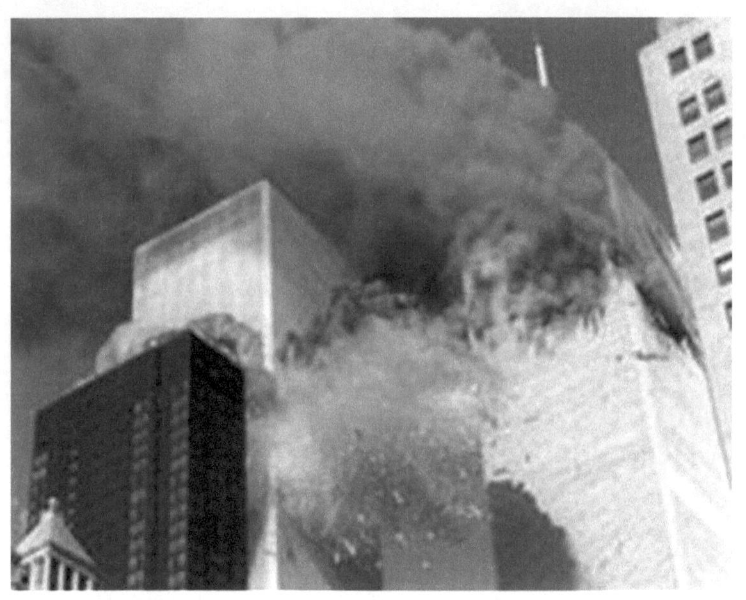

FRONTISPIECE
BACK TO EARTH
LIFE AND DEATH WITHOUT EGO

Dedication

To Father Mychal Judge, OFM, who was a brother to my Franciscan brother, Alphonse, in more ways than one. Father Mychal was the first responder to 9/11/2001 who met the Real God.

To my wife, Margaret (Peggy) Crehan, who still hasn't read all of my books, but Love is much better than reading.

To Annette Castello Wilcox who has joined her beloved Jack in the Eternal Now.

To my beloved brother, Guy, who is in a much, much better place in the Oneness of Being

To Bob and Pat Willis who have been an inspiration forever. We are One in the Spirit

And, of course, once more, to Pierre Teilhard DeChardin, the Jesuit mystic, who is a Jesus, and a Buddha, and a Lao Tsu for me.

Epigraph

"If, as a result of some interior revolution, I were to lose in succession my faith in Christ, my faith in a personal God, and my faith in spirit, I feel that I should continue to believe invincibly in the world. The world (its value, its infallibility and its goodness.)—that, when all is said and done, is the first, the last, and the only thing in which I believe. It is by this faith that I live. And it is to this faith, I feel that at the moment of death, rising above all doubts, I shall surrender myself."

Teilhard DeChardin, *Christianity and Evolution*, p.99

Prominent in this book is Teilhard's famous saying: "We are not human beings having a spiritual experience, but we are spiritual beings having a human experience."

Indeed, Pierre, we are coming back to your beloved earth to join you in the Oneness of Being at the Omega Point in the Eternal Now.

Acknowledgements

I would like to thank everybody and everything who has ever acknowledged my existence. Thanks for making me feel so alive.

I thank all those who read my first two books and encouraged me to write a third.

I thank all those who ignored my first two books and thus encouraged me to write a third.

I thank especially those who disagreed with my first two books, and thus encouraged me to write a third. (Fuggeddaboudit! This is my last.)

I would like to thank all those on my E-mail address book, especially the members of AECR@yahoogroups.com; our Home Mass Group; my cousins, other relatives, and friends: former Redemptorists, active Redemptorists; Movement For a Better World members; Corpus, FCM, Rentapriest.com, Omega Group, golf club members, tennis club members, 70+ski club members, whew, I didn't realize what a joiner I am!

I would like to thank my two Shihtzus, Mikey and Charley, who patiently sat and waited for months while I wrote. Talk about loyalty, commitment, and love!

I apologize to all my cherished friends who are atheists, theists, agnostics, Unitarian Universalists, Humanists, Jews, Muslims, and Hindus, for my insistence on giving my most cherished Jewish friend, Jesus, a prominent place in these books.

Lastly, I give a very special thanks to Bishop John Shelby Spong, Ekhart Tolle, Jan Kersschott, Roger Haight, Dominic Crossan, Marcus Borg, Karen Armstrong, and all the authors in my three Bibliographies. Please read them, even if you choose to skip my writings, but especially if you choose to skip my writings.

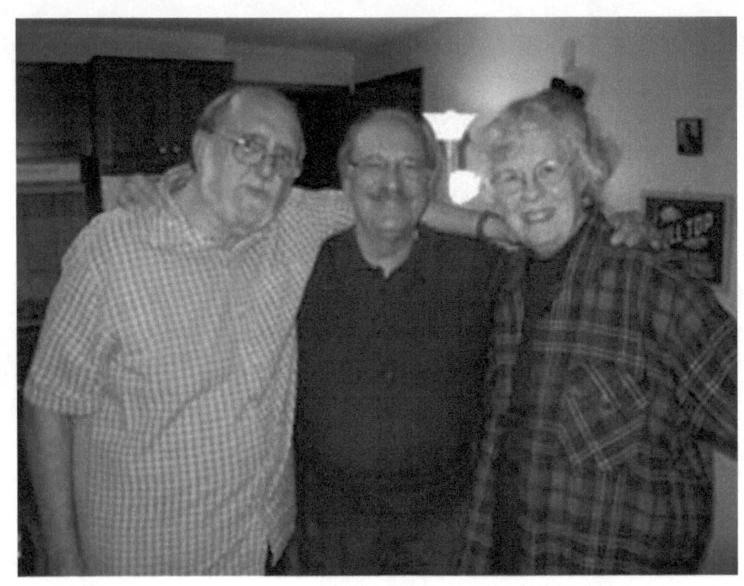

BOB WILLIS, SAL UMANA AND PAT WILLIS

Foreword by Bob Willis

T HERE ARE DAYS. All peoples have them. They slice sharp lines between before and after. They deliver shocks through the firmament of the moment, creating fissures that shatter security, summoning ghosts into and expelling them out from their graves. Depending upon where one stands, we name them. On April 19, 1775, a shot rang out, heard round the world. Within eight years a new nation conceived in liberty emerged from the stinking fog of war: a Rebellion or a Revolution? Eight decades later under the red glare of rockets a battle of brothers erupted, threatening unity and challenging freedom: a War of Secession or a Civil War? No one living in America in 1929 could doubt that the Great Depression had swallowed up the Roaring Twenties: a tragedy, or a payback for societal sin? It ended when a day of infamy roused a sleeping giant and unleashed a world-changing maelstrom of technological slaughter: a salvaging of pride but for whom? Oh, some days.

Some welcomed in the third Christian millennium as the Age of America; others plotted the infidel's demise. From Western ashes the phoenix of Mohammed would rise. Firebirds plunged out of unblinking heavens; the giant tumbled to its knees; the land trembled, then sobbed. As the stones of Yahweh had vanquished massive Goliath, so the missiles of Allah tore open their symbolic targets. A cataclysmic fault line appeared: for us, the darkness of the Age of Terrorism; for bin Laden and acolytes, the dawning of the Rebirth of Islam.

How to respond? As the holy man inquires, "What seek ye: the regaining of security, the restoring of power, or the furthering of life?

Striving For Security

Since dawn first peeked through the enveloping darkness, earthbound humans supplicated the heavens above. Recognizing the vast disparity between the immortals and themselves, they devised various strategies to garner special favor. To jealous gods they offered their first and best fruits, from loins to fields. With the fickle and arbitrary they employed flattery, evasiveness, and gestures of obeisance. In response to eternal kingship they pledged obedience, loyalty, and tireless efforts in expanding the kingdom. Paul, a new Christian, spoke to humankind when he assured his Roman audience: "If God is with us, who is against us?" Jesus, as God's son, went further, counseling calmness before adversity: "Fear not, it is I . . . I will not leave you orphans . . . if I do not go away, the Counselor will not come to you; but if I go I will send him to you."

In critical moments frantic humans redoubled their pleas for divine intervention: by virgin sacrifices and burnt offerings; public parades of repentance, with itchy sackcloth and irritating ashes leading mournful sinners onward toward painful flagellations and even cruel crucifixions; ceaseless prayers, midnight vigils, punishing fasts and elaborate rituals; and always promises . . . promises . . . promises of increased devotion and reinvigorated goodness. At times the floods receded; sometimes diseases disappeared; moments even occurred when dictators fell and bombs stopped falling and savagery ceased. Thank god!

Most often relief came after the bloodiest of journeys. Religious belief and practice did not spare an estimated one third of Christian Europe that perished from the Bubonic Plague in the 14th Century. The worship of earthen deities did little to protect America's Indians over three devastating centuries from killings, forced removal, and the callous disregard of invading Europeans. Yahweh seemed to abandon the millions of Europe's Jews who perished day after day after day under Nazi tyranny. The Christian Trinity did not mitigate the excruciating march of agony after the fall of Corregidor for wounded, exhausted, and dying Filipinos and Americans. Neither did ancestor worship nor discipleship of Buddha shield the 70,000 men, women, and children

166

of Hiroshima from a blinding flash of horror. Nor did its faith save Nagasaki's Christian population from incineration.

No matter the reasons proposed for perceived divine inaction, the fact remains: one risks all that terror can produce if one banks on the gods for security on earth. Perhaps humans must look to their own resources for protection from enemies

SAFETY THROUGH FORCE

As of the present, death ultimately wins. Humankind congenitally pursues strategies to defeat it: discovering and drinking from the fountain of youth, slowing the process of aging, manufacturing durable body replacements for fleshy ones subject to deterioration and exhaustion, pioneering powerful drugs to overcome disease, perfecting brilliant surgical interventions to preserve, heal, and re-grow our biological being. Some even dream of resurrection and reincarnation (usually with non-earthly assistance). Without foreclosing the possible, one forecasts the probable: no one can, nor will, evade the grim grasp of death, at least eventually. Safety from death?—no.

Death utilizes natural catastrophes to wipe out significant portions of humanity in this time, this place. Earthquakes shatter and tsunamis overwhelm. Tornadoes level and hurricanes uproot. Wind-lashed fires consume with indiscriminate abandon. Pitiless heat parches the screaming earth, dries up sustaining waters, shrivels vital food supplies, enervates and kills. Human ingenuity has sharpened means of prediction; it also has devised methods of lessening disasters' rampages. On the whole, however, human beings, favoring short-term fixes and immediate protection, intervene in ways that promise future, more devastating, more widespread environmental disruptions. Given the stubborn denial of humanity's negative impact on the earth's life-sustaining capacity, a reasonable person predicts ongoing and increasing life-destroying natural events. Only the unlikely reign of intelligent and foreseeing leaders and the disappearance of individual, tribal, and national greed may spare us from nature's terrors.

Which leaves only stopgap strategies to forestall human-fomented terrorism: to kill, to imprison, and to exclude.

Aspiring empires field the finest of armies fitted out with ever-more ferocious weapons. They snuff out terror through terror. Sometimes they succeed: "Little Boy" and "Fat Man" brought a trembling emperor and his cowed generals to defeated knees. Sometimes they fail: industrial America, technologically mighty and embarrassingly rich, finally bowed down, and out, before the proud determination of an agricultural Peoples' Army. Immediate victory may occur as when the Allies conquered Germany on the battlefield and humiliated it at Versailles. But thereby they planted the killing fields of a Second World War. America prevailed there also but provoked the prolonged stress of a Cold War. It watched gleefully and with an attitude of "I told you so" as the Soviet Union split apart. But now rogue nations like Iran and Pakistan and North Korea, and guerrilla forces like al Queda and its fundamentalist allies, conspire to use against us the nuclear weapons we created. No doubt, force may overpower this hour's foe; it fathers, however, a future of tomorrow's antagonists. "He who lives by the sword will die by the sword."

Throughout recorded history resourceful protectors of their own have erected walls to keep dissidents either in or out. To isolate the disturbing, despotic rulers situate gulags deep in forsaken interiors: America for its Indians, Germany for its Jews, Bolsheviks for all non-believers in Stalinist Communism, America for its own Japanese-Americans. Consider this: with five percent of the world's population, the United States incarcerates 2.3 million people or nearly one quarter of the total prison population on our planet. During the Cold War, European Communism threw up the Berlin Wall in a desperate attempt to keep a whole population from fleeing its jurisdiction. "Mr. Gorbachev, tear down this wall." On the other hand, democratic rulers tend to erect barriers to entrance rather than for escape. One need only recall the 344 miles of fence currently separating California, Arizona, New Mexico, and some of Texas from neighboring Mexico. Only a high, wire-topped, electronically-guarded, and drone—patrolled barricade will keep the drug runners and illegal immigrants from flowing into our land, so pronounces the current wisdom. Or call to mind the layers of surveillance in our airports, all designed by the Department of Homeland Security to keep terrorists at bay.

Do walls work? Sometimes . . . until someone figures how to tunnel under them, or vault over them, or wiggle through them. Do walls work? Sometimes . . . until the fort's ramparts feel like a prison's suffocating grip. After all, who really is safer than someone in solitary confinement? What do we want: security or freedom?

THE FREEDOM OF LIVING

If we should not put good money on heavenly protection, if we should not rely on governments to save us in this age of danger, whither on earth should we turn? This author, a modern mystic with twinkling eyes, shares his answer. He describes for us a path he has long trod, going back and forth, breathing deeply of life's treasures while mapping the way. Read on. His vision may fill out, expand, and deepen your own. Perhaps best of all, you may expect to experience with him and in him and through him delight-filled ripples of joy.

Robert J. Willis, Ph.D. Sequim, Washington, July 2011

Introduction

ON SATURDAY AFTERNOON, September 8, 2001, I stood at the Eighteenth Green of Pebble Beach Golf Course on the Monterey Peninsula of California. It had been a perfect Pacific Coast golf day, temperature around 50 degrees Fahrenheit. (I had heard that most of the homeowners at Pebble Beach owned summer homes further inland to escape the cold of the coast. The winter, of course, is the same as the summer on that coast. Oh well, the people who lived at Pebble Beach could afford a summer home.)

What was I doing on the Eighteenth hole of Pebble Beach? Certainly not completing a round of golf in the Pro-Am tournament, not with my US Golf Association Handicap Index of 31.5. I was dressed in a white ministerial robe and white stole to officiate at a wedding. The bride and groom were from London, England, and the mother of the groom had a home at Pebble Beach. I was billeted at the home of a former U.S. Women's champion tennis player. The guests were about 200 very successful people from all five continents. You asked, what was a 5 ft., 7 inch Sicilian doing at an affair of this proportion? My niece, Ann Crehan, from Baltimore, MD was best friends with the sister of the groom.

As I stood on the platform which was decorated in white roses, I was facing southeast with the sun and the Pacific on my right, and in front of me, the huge blue expanse of Monterey Bay, the seals and their rocks, and their breaking billows, and the green mountains of the California coast filling the horizon. I have to say, it looked almost as spectacular as the coast of Sicily, where my parents were born, and if it wasn't so freezing cold I might have sprung for that 300 dollar round of golf at 5:00 AM on Monday which was offered to me. This, of course, was a huge discount offered to clergy—everybody else had to pay 500 dollars and make reservations at least three months in advance. After the bagpiper led us to the five chef (imported Japanese) sushi cocktail hour, I was very grateful to retire to my room in the professional tennis player's home.

On Sunday, we were all guests at the Post-Wedding Brunch over in Carmel, and then my best friends, Ron and Mary Ann Bastian, picked me up and brought me to their home in Salinas. On Monday, September 10, we visited the incredible, state of the art, John Steinbeck museum in Salinas. I did not know it then, but one of the great American writers fired up my imagination and set the stage for my once in a lifetime literary (?), achievement, namely, this Twin Towers Trilogy. Of course, it was all part of the stage setting for the most life-transforming event of my seventy one years: the Sept. 11,2001 attack by Osama Bin Laden, of unhappy memory, and his jihadi lads.

On Tuesday morning, September 11, my bags were packed and waiting by the door and I was eating breakfast before leaving for Monterey Air and the flight to San Francisco and my departure finally to JFK, New York. Breakfast was not exactly at Tiffany's but about 70 blocks south, at the World Trade Center in Lower Manhattan. I remember Pearl Harbor, Dec. 7, 1941, and the days when John F. Kennedy, Martin Luther King, Jr., and Robert F. Kennedy were shot. They all left an indelible scar on my soul for which there is no healing. But the suicide bombing on 9/11/01 by Muslim fundamentalists using our own jet planes, left an open wound that can never be closed as long as I live. Even though our crack commandos of Navy Seal Team 6 celebrated the tenth anniversary of the attack on the Trade Center by taking revenge on Osama Bin Laden in Pakistan on May Day, 2011, the gaping wound in Lower Manhattan is forever a reminder of how vulnerable are our bodies and our souls in this the Age of Terrorism.

After that fateful "Breakfast at the Twin Towers," President George W. Bush, of course, closed all the airports in the United States, inflicting more pain and misery on our American citizens. It was the beginning of our capitulation to Al Qaeda. We surrendered to the terrorists by allowing fear to frighten us and destroy our peace of mind and our freedom, and we hypocritically masked that fear in a phony "War on Terrorism" that has become the longest war ever fought by the U.S., and it is designed from its very premises to last forever. As long as you tell us that we have to "Kill them over there', so they won't kill us over here, you have committed yourself to a lifetime of silly, technical, military-industrial complex wars that have already bankrupted our nation.

After that fateful Tuesday, and a useless trip to San Francisco to board a flight, or bus, or train to New York, we waited four days until Friday, when my friend Ron Bastian gassed up his panel truck and said, "Let's drive to New York." Ron had driven across the country dozens of times, and was supremely up to the task. It was a sixty hour trip, around the clock, without stopping to sleep. We tried to sleep in a motel the first night, but after all the coffee we were drinking, we both lay there, sleepless, for about an hour, then jumped up together and said, "Let's go," and never slept again except for an occasional nap in a Restaurant Parking lot. As a matter of fact, I have never had a complete 6 hour sleep at night since that fateful time.

It was a journey worthy of Steinbeck's "Travels With Charley." Everywhere we went across the country there were signs of a nation quivering and cowering under siege. Texas, especially, was covered with "Don't Mess With Texas " bravado" signs in honor of our cowboy President "W" who vowed to "go after the despicable cowards who were threatening us," and "Bring It On", and "25 million dollars for anyone of these jihadists pictured on this deck of cards." Oklahoma City was notable for being all lit up around the scene where the biggest attack by domestic terrorists had occurred. It enhanced the feeling that no one was safe or secure any more. America was surrounded by fanatics who hated us within and without. When, finally, we crossed the Verrazano-Narrows Bridge from Staten Island to Brooklyn, and looked north towards Manhattan, our hearts sunk. All we could see by the lights were fire and smoke, and, of course, the toxic grey cloud of dust containing the splattered and exploded remains of three thousand human bodies. But what about their souls, I thought, what about their souls? All the religions of the NY, NJ, and CT Metropolitan area said their souls were all with God. But where was God?

CHAPTER I
THE GOD WHO NEVER WAS

IN THE DAYS and weeks after the Twin Towers shuddered and collapsed, I had several mystical experiences. I am in the habit of daily meditation, and there was never anything like the holocaust of three thousand innocent victims of insane terrorism to put my unconscious in touch with ultimate reality. I saw in meditation the fire from thousands of gallons of jet fuel so hot that it melted the tons of steel girders that held up the tallest skyscrapers the world had ever seen. Over and over again, I felt myself sitting in the "Windows On the World" atop one of the towers, where I had a cocktail when dating my wife, where I brought my cousins from Italy to see one of the greatest views on earth, where I performed many weddings with my Cantor and Rabbi friends. On my mystical magic carpet from Ground Zero where the Towers once stood, I flew instantaneously through my entire life's experience of God. I knew intuitively that the God the jihad fundamentalists believed in was a fraud.

During my many meditations after 9/11 I could not actually see the smoke rising above Ground Zero from my home in Freeport, Long Island, 24 miles southeast of Lower Manhattan. But my soul could see the smoke just as clearly as the smoke from Auschwitz and the other gas ovens of the European holocaust, along with the nuclear mushroom clouds above Hiroshima and Nagasaki from my own "Greatest Generation's" "Good" War. I also saw the smoke from the Dow Chemical napalm holocaust of the Vietnam War, (called the "American War" in Vietnam) where we dropped more tonnage of bombs on Vietnam and Cambodia than we had on Germany in World War II.

It was all part of an obscene, unspeakable chaos that was challenging the stability of my Cosmos, along with the sanity of my soul. When your Cosmos collapses to whom do you turn? The ancient Greeks had a god called Cosmos, which literally meant "the beautiful" that is, the entire beautiful clockwork of the surrounding universe, especially at night. But they had another god called "Chaos" who symbolized the unspeakable horror of total death and destruction of the Cosmos. Since the Greeks were much smarter than us, I decided in my meditations to let Cosmos and Chaos fight it out among themselves. It didn't work.

After two thousand years we had supposedly rid ourselves of Greek mythology and pagan idols because we had a real God who actually was "Our Father in heaven" who was on our side, the People of God's side, whoever we happened to call ourselves at the moment. Our Heavenly Father was supposed to protect us from evil and from all the sinister forces that would try to destroy our Cosmos, because he was infinite and omnipotent, and so personal that he knew each one of us by name.

Where was our Heavenly Father now? The smoke over Ground Zero became for me in my meditations like the smoke over the Temple of Jerusalem in 70 A.D. when many devout Jews knew for sure that the Hebrew Yaweh had died in the destruction of the Temple and the Ark of the Covenant. My soul cried out, "What happened to Our Father in Heaven?" To whom do you pray at the Grave of the God of Monotheism? How can you have a Requiem for the God you believed in and prayed to every day of your life? How do you preside at the funeral of God? Since the God I grew up with was dead, and since I had to have some God to make any sense out of this chaotic world we live in, I imagined a "whatever" God comes to me, a low-end Social Work psychotherapist, with a nervous breakdown because she/he/it has lost her identity and wants to find out under my questionable "therapy" who she/he/it really is. So I wrote a book about my mystical experience of the death of God, called "The Day God Died: How the Twin Towers Became the Grave of the God of Monotheism". I was the lucky therapist that God came to with an identity crisis, and in the course of the treatment, both God and Her therapist found out stuff about God that neither of us never knew. (sic. With or without the 'k'.)

When I published "The Day God Died", everybody except my four or five best friends was outraged. They were angry because they said it was a typical Sal Umana provocation just to startle people to attention. How can you talk about the death of God? How could the very source of life itself have died? But they missed the point. What I was saying was that the God that most people believed in not only died, but never really existed. Try telling this to someone who spent their whole life worshipping, serving, fearing, thanking, and beseeching a God who never really existed at all. Believers had made such an idol, such a world-class, indeed, Cosmic class, solid gold graven image of God that they were totally dependent upon in time and in eternity, that they could not conceive of the possibility that he had died. Not only, but that he never even existed, even as an image of Divinity. So I tried to tell them that their God never existed, and I was close to being burned at the stake. It's one thing to tell kids there's no Santa Claus, but quite another to tell grownups, especially of the traditionalist, fundamentalist variety, that their 'Cosmic Papa' never existed at all. We are talking about the omnipotent, omniscient Lord God Almighty who created the world out of nothing, and who holds it all together, and who made man in his own image and likeness, indeed, as the psalmist says, made us 'a little less than the angels'.

I now remember a transformative experience while visiting the Sistine Chapel in Rome in November, 2004. It was a time of heightened awareness for me because the Boston Red Sox had swept the St. Louis Cardinals to win their first World Series in almost a century. I was with my best friends, Bill and Rafa O'Hara, and my wife Peggy, suffering from neck strain, gazing at the greatest painting in history that told the story of God's relationship with mankind. Michelangelo had spent seven years symbolizing God's relationship with us. He depicts God as the red robed, white bearded 'Cosmic Papa' coming out of eternal darkness to create sun, moon, and stars, and in the following scene he hurls out the globe of earth and is in such a hurry to get around the earth and create us, the center of his darling tenderness, that God's robe falls off and shows us the crack of his buttocks, literally, moons the universe, to get to earth and put out his divine finger to draw Adam's finger out of the clay of this planet. Did Michelangelo follow the conventional wisdom of his day, and think that the sun, and moon, and stars, all revolved around us? It doesn't matter, Michelangelo was a true renaissance man and undoubtedly a mystic, who knew that his seven year torture painting those frescoes upside down, so well described in "The Agony and the Ecstasy", were just a metaphor for the love affair with divinity with which every human being is born.

That love affair with the God who always was and always will be is the subject of Chapter II, and hopefully Michelangelo's magnificent masterpiece of metaphor will become part of a museum that includes the entire Vatican Basilica along with the remains of a wonderful institution that has finally purged itself of idolatry, and followed literally the words of its egalitarian Jewish mystic founder, and understood divinity as Jesus did, 'in spirit and in truth', with the literal beatitudes, by loving one another as the only way we human animals can transcend our evolutionary 'survival of the fittest' gene. That is the day when we will understand that the only divinity we will know in person is to love and be loved in return, as in an old song from the forty's, "Nature Boy", which I sang as a fourteen year old. But for now, we must still talk about the 'Cosmic Papa Santa Claus', the golden idol, we all believed in as emotional, needy children, and whom we now know, never really was. Never, ever, really was . . . .

As I wrote in my first book, under "Doing Therapy for God", what was left of my concept of God came to me on the Second Sunday after the Twin towers collapse:

"God came to me this morning and asked for a therapy session. I told her, 'Why are you coming to me? This afternoon at 2:30 PM there will be a huge religious service at Yankee Stadium. The Cardinal Archbishop of NY will be there, all the other Bishops from the metropolitan area will be there. All the Protestant and Orthodox leaders will be there. The Jewish Rabbis: Orthodox, Conservative, Reformed, even the Hassidim will be there. The Imams from all the Muslim Mosques, even from Malcom (X) Shabazz will be there. The Hindus, the Sikh's, the Shinto's, the Buddhists, even the Pagan Druids will be there, even the Chinese who believe that you are their grandmother will be there. Go there and you will feel better.'

"It was then that God broke out into uncontrollable weeping. She shook so bad I thought she was having a nervous breakdown. Then she began, 'Sure, they'll all be there, and they will be everywhere in the world: the believers in me. The Muslims, who call themselves Islam: the People of God; the Jews, who call themselves the Chosen People of you know Who; the Christians who call themselves the People of God; all the people of the earth who acknowledge me as Earth Mother, Creator, Higher Power, Great Spirit, Whatever, Whatever. They all regard themselves as my children. But they have spent all of history hating each other, hurting each other, killing each other. It's bad enough that they do this to each other, but why do they have to do it in My Name?

"God then broke into even deeper sobs, and I really was afraid she was going to lose it. So I tried to distract her with this little ditty to the tune of 'America the Beautiful". I told her that even though I was a Christian, I could still sing this song for my Muslim brothers and sisters:

> *"(Salaam means Peace)*
> *Salaam, Islam, Salaam Islam*
> *"Allah be good to you.*
> *"To Arabs all, and Farsi, too,*
> *"All Muslims black and brown,*
> *"Allah look down, bless all of you,*
> *"And give you Peace at home.*
> *"Salaam, Islam, Salaam, Islam*
> *"Allah be good to you."*

"At first God thought I might be losing it myself with the likes of this little ditty, then she calmed down a little bit, and seemed to be okay for the moment. But what do I tell her when she comes back for her next session?"

I sent this first therapy session out as an E-mail to my friends and relatives. Some thought that I had flipped my lid and was suffering from PTSD, seriously; some thought that it was just a joke; some said that I should turn this into a book. So I wrote a therapy session for God once a week for the next fourteen weeks. I meditated on that Yankee Stadium event which was probably the biggest outwardly religious ecumenical gathering in our nation's history. All the religions were there and assured all the relatives and friends of the deceased that their beloved martyrs were all with God. But where was God? The God most of the religious leaders were talking about was having an identity crisis so bad that She was in danger of becoming an atheist. For God's sake, She couldn't believe in Herself! The God most monotheists believed in, especially of the three Abrahamic faiths: Judaism, Christianity, and Islam, was sadly a God who never existed in the way they portrayed God to be.

As I pondered the traumatic events around 9/11 and the response of the American people to them, and indeed the response of the entire world, I realized how transforming this event was becoming, and for no one more than myself. As a mystic, I see everything in relation to God, which is another name for Ultimate Reality in my unconscious mind. It is the transcendent/ immanent power that is the basis of all reality and holds the world together. I had been immersed for several years in Thomas Berry and Brian Swimme's books: " The Universe Story: A Celebration of the Unfolding of the Cosmos", and "The Hidden Heart of the Cosmos: Humanity and the New Story", and "The Dream of the Earth." They try to tell the story that we human beings are responsible for all life on earth, and that we have to treat earth as a living being: the 'Gaia,' the earth as mother, which gave life to us all. They were followers of Teilhard DeChardin, a Jesuit Mystic, who believed in the earth itself as Our Heavenly Mother. Those are my words, not Teilhard's, but they try to say what Teilhard meant. Now, as I contemplated the atrocities perpetrated by Osama Bin Laden and his Jihadists, I could not help but think they did all these as an act of worship and martyrdom for their version of God. I saw right away that this would dig a huge dent in the non-Muslim world's perception of the Muslim Allah/God. Even though the jihadists were a very tiny minority of Muslim believers, any concept of God that would sanction the killing of one's self along with the slaughter of innocent bystanders had to be a sick concept indeed. As a mystic who experiences God intuitively every day, I knew immediately that any concept of a God who would sanction such slaughter in his name had to be a very primitive tribal concept!

But what was my dismay when the American President, George W. bush, in the name of his version of God, declared a war of "infinite justice" to go to Afghanistan to kill Al Qaeda and the Taliban fundamentalists who harbored them! The American President based this act of aggression toward our human brothers on his concept of God: divine justice toward anybody who wanted to attack us! Who was the God of Bin Laden, and who was the God of George Bush? Neither of them was the God I grew up with in South Boston. I was taught in Sunday School by the Sisters of Charity of Nazareth, Kentucky, that God was Our Father in Heaven. In their southern accents they told us that it was all in the Baltimore Catechism which they handed out. We were the children of God, and He made us to know Him, and love Him, and serve Him in this world and be happy with him forever in the next.

When we were growing up, all Catholics throughout the world, indeed, most Christians, internalized this image of God, as the existential theologian, Paul Tillich calls Him: the Cosmic Papa, the old man with the white beard, kind of a super Santa of the Universe. He was the one we talked to whenever we needed something, especially something big, like a change in the weather, or help in the final exams. I later called Him "the Go-for God", chiding those who used God for a Divine errand boy. After the Twin Towers attack, I immediately wondered what had happened to this benign, kindly old omnipotent Super Grandpa. Was he on vacation when these strange Muslim martyrs spent a few years attending American aviation schools with the explicit plan of high-jacking jumbo jets at the beginning of transcontinental flights so they could crash a full load of fuel into the tallest skyscrapers in the world, and also the U.S. Capital, and the Pentagon, simultaneously? Who was this God they were praying to seven times a day to enable them to kill as many infidels as possible?

Thus I did an imaginary course of psychotherapy on my imaginary concept of God, at least the God I had grown up with and had served as a Catholic Priest for 35 years. In the course of this psychotherapy, I found out that the God I grew up with had a real identity problem. He could no longer be identified with the God of the fundamentalists of the three mainstream monotheistic religions. But it turned out to be my own identity problem, for I had identified myself all my life as a seeker of God, and in asking "Who was this God?" I was really asking who was I, since I had identified all my life as a 'seeker of God'. So it was really therapy for myself, or as Freud would have called it: a self-analysis. It is interesting to note that after I sent 'The Day God Died' to my therapist, he wrote me a blistering critique in which he said that only Sal Umana could be so grandiose and filled with hubris that he would consider doing therapy for God! He also remarked that he was very sorry that I had lost my faith in the divinity of Jesus Christ. But I told him, as I had to tell countless others that Jesus could not possibly be God, because God Himself wasn't God anymore! This got me in trouble more than anything else I ever said or wrote, simply because you have to understand what the word God can mean.

First of all, we have to agree on the general meaning of the word 'God'. If we are constantly talking about God and we have different, unshared meanings for the word God, there is no way we can understand the concepts about God that do not fit a common shared meaning for the word 'God.' First of all, we are only talking about the Anglo-Saxon word 'God', and if we say God with a capital 'G' we usually mean the universal God, not a god with a lower case 'g', who is usually one of a pantheon of gods in whatever mythology you happen to be discussing at the time. Also, very important, capital 'G' God is not necessarily a separate being from the visible universe, which theists believe in. God could also be part of visible reality, indeed, God could be the Ground of Being, whatever that means, or simply Being Itself, or the Spirit (which means life-breath) of the universe, whether visible or invisible universe. Now before this gets completely out of hand, let's return to the word 'God.'

Long before humans could talk, they could feel and sense intuitively that there was a force, a power, a life-giving breath/spirit (same word) that they had to respect, and pay attention to. When man began to speak, one of the first words he used was 'God', which referred to some kind of 'libation', or 'sacrifice' to please the hidden power up until now only known intuitively, or unconsciously. Carl Jung, the Swiss psychologist, and inventor of the 'collective unconscious' talks about all peoples from earliest pre-history having unconscious symbols in their dreams which they acted out consciously when they awakened. It was all part of human evolution. Jung pictures one of the earliest humans coming out of his cave at dawn and looking at the glowing red globe of the rising sun and recognizing it as a symbol of the higher power in the sky. Early man must have raised his arms in a gesture of awe and worship, and eventually made a 'libation', or a 'sacrifice to the higher power', which he called 'god'. So a 'god' was something you made sacrifices to as an act of worship. Whether you actually made a libation by drinking something and/or poured it on the earth, or sacrificed an animal by burning it or eating it, you were worshiping the higher power you wanted to placate or petition. For our purposes here, we will skip about ten thousand years or so of religious history, and talk about the word 'God' with a capital 'G', because 'god' with a small 'g' takes us too far afield. We are talking here about the One God, the universal God, the Lord God Almighty, Creator of Heaven and Earth that all the monotheistic faiths worship.

It would be easy to join the well-publicized atheists, (whom I will not mention) and scoff at the God that most atheists presume people of faith worship. Karen Armstrong in her absolutely perfect "The Case For God" (Alfred A. Knopf, NY, Toronto, 2009) points out (p.305)that these 'new' atheists set up a straw man of people of faith and confuse faith with belief. Faith for atheists becomes the 'root of all evil' because once believers accept something on faith that can have no scientific proof, then they can believe anything they are taught about God, no matter how absurd. As I will explain later in Chapter 2, I distinguish between faith and belief. Faith, when it is a blind assent of the mind, especially when it is against reason and science, is hardly better than childish faith in Santa Claus. Whereas belief, in the old Anglo-Saxon meaning of be-love, is a commitment in love to the Higher Power whoever or whatever it may be that one experiences daily in their unconscious intuition.

For now, we are talking about "The God who never was," and clearly God is not the "Pie in the sky" Grandpa Santa Claus for adults who can climb down non-existent chimneys and fulfill our wish lists. Is God the Great Accountant, keeping book on our every secret thought and kinky desire, and just waiting to punish us with fire when we die? Millions of people still believe God is such a punisher. None of them will ever read this book, so I am spared the unpleasant task of discussing that God. Besides, I spent the first thirty five years or so of my life believing in and preaching that God on Redemptorist Missions. In fact, I was sent to Italy for a year to learn Italian and preach Missions in Italy as they had done for the past three hundred years. Every Thursday night was on "Judgement and Hell", and I had to give a thirty minute sermon on it, in English or Italian, when I returned to the U.S. I'll never get out of my mind that little sparrow who comes around every year and brushes its little wing against this solid metal ball made up of all the planets in the solar system, (including Pluto, that dog, who has since been demoted to a large asteroid) and when that little sparrow, coming once a year, finally brushes away the last final grain of metal from that huge ball of brass, after Billions and Billions of Years, you'll still be burning in hell! And of course: the Fires of Hell! Here, put your little finger on this cigarette lighter, and hold it there – now, how would you like to have your whole body stuck in a bonfire like Joan of Arc, and she didn't really mind it that much because she was on her way to heaven, but you are gonna burn down here for ALL ETERNITY! A BLESSING WHICH I WISH UPON YOUSE ALL, In the Name of the Father, and of the Son, and of the Holy Ghost. Amen. (Want to hear it in Italian?)

A recent op-ed article in the New York Times by Robert Douthat gives the typical conservative argument in favor of hell. If everybody goes to heaven what about the evil people who don't want to go to heaven? Don't they have free will, why punish them with heaven when they see people as hell? I submit that the silliness of this traditional argument is proved by the new thinking that there is neither a heaven nor a hell place after death. The so-called heaven or hell place is right here, before death. We do indeed have free will, and there is absolutely no predestination. We freely decide right now whether people are heaven or people are hell, and we are living in either one of those places right now. It's your call. And what happens to your spirit/self after your body dies is beyond my level of competence to speculate. Again, you're on your own.

Back in the 70's, a very popular book went around called "The God I Don't Believe In" by Juan Arias. This Spanish writer told of his personal feelings about God from the negative point of view, namely, what he definitely did not believe about God. At the time, I was giving retreats in Catholic Parishes and presented this idea as an exercise for sharing faith in large groups. There were two parts to this exercise: in part one, we shared our ideas about the God we did NOT believe in, and in part two, we talked about the God we DID believe in. This was 35 years ago, and even though that counts for many centuries in this era of the knowledge explosion since the birth of the computer, already there were intimations that many people were beginning to discard the ancient and medieval ideas about God that were being taught whether formally or informally in the Catholic Church. But since the 70's and especially since the birth of the Personal Computer, and the new scriptural, theological, and psychological scholarship it bred, there has been an almost infinite explosion of change in the field of faith. Now especially in the New Millennium, with the exponential rise in fundamentalism and suicidal fanaticism exemplified by the Twin Towers Attacks, questions are being asked, hundreds of books are being written, and the media are full of discussions about what these religious fanatics are thinking. Karen Armstrong in "The Battle For God" has what I think is the best study of the rise of fundamentalism, especially among the Muslims. But as she explains so well, all religions are suffering from the ridicule of their Sacred Books, and the contradictions within their own scriptures, and in comparison to other scriptures. People with only a rudimentary knowledge of religion can see that there is something wrong when the Universal God turns out to have especially chosen the Jews, and then especially chosen the Christians, and then especially chosen the Muslims, then the Mormons, then the Jehovah's Witnesses, then the Seventh Day Adventists, not to mention the Shinto's. The knowledge explosion in the age of technology has put all traditional religions on the defensive. You can't have multiple "One True Religions" organized and institutionalized as the "One true faith."Either their idea of God has to change, or their idea of who they are in relation to God has to change. All religions are on the defensive, according to Karen Armstrong, and worse, they suffer from the threat of annihilation, if enough followers begin to doubt the authenticity and historicity of their sacred myths and stories. In her 'Brief History of Myth' Armstrong tries to explain the crucial difference between myths, metaphors, and symbols of eternal truth and 'Logos' which is the realistic acceptance of what logical facts and events are in reality.

Especially in the field of Judeo-Christian Sacred Scriptures, modern Biblical Scholarship has debunked a very large portion of the historical accuracy of both the Old and the New Testaments. Bishop John Shelby Spong in "The Sins of Scripture" makes a superbly challenging case for the abuse of Scripture by both Jews and Christians to justify all kinds of offenses against humanity in the name of God. "How can a book called 'The Word of God' leave a trail of such violence, hostility, and death throughout history?"No wonder fundamentalists feel threatened by modern biblical scholarship.

Moving on further, the God I no longer believe in is the God of the Last Judgment. Traditional Christian teaching pictures God separating the goats from the sheep, and sending the goats to hell while welcoming the sheep to heaven. It is a very stark and candid judgment on human behavior. Nothing could say more clearly how right it is to treat your neighbor as yourself, and how wrong it is to ignore all those who are less fortunate than you. It may well be the greatest ethical teaching in history, but when taken literally as the 'Word of God,' and applied to teachings on heaven and hell, it loses its deeper meaning. The Jewish peasant, Jesus, never talked about a future life, because he only knew about THIS life, and when he said you have to treat your neighbor as yourself, he did not mean "so that you will be happy in some future life after death."Jesus was talking about happiness in THIS life, and all you have to do is look at the people who ignore their fellow man and ask yourself how much contentment and peace of heart they can possibly have. I leave it to others to document this point, because I have wasted too much of my life arguing with the greedy and the selfish about how unhappy they are even though they think they are having an infinitely better time than me!

To conclude this Chapter on the "God Who Never Was," I would like to quote from the Thirteenth Therapy Session in "The Day God Died".

"I decided to attack God's identity problem head on. I asked Her., 'What do you think is wrong with You?'

"I know that this is a stupid question, and I would never use it with a human patient, but after all She is God, so I felt that She could take it.

"God said, 'If I knew what was wrong with Me, I wouldn't need therapy would I?' She answered smartly. 'You're the therapist, what do YOU think is wrong with Me?'

"'You are having an identity crisis' I answered. 'But don't worry, it's very age appropriate. We all reach a point in life where we need to know who we are, as opposed to anyone else.'

"'What's wrong with the answer I gave Moses?', She retorted, 'I'm Me,' She actually sounded like a teenage girl when She said it.

I'm sorry, God, but you know that wasn't an answer. Who are You, as opposed to everyone else and everything else in the universe, as opposed to the Universe itself?"

"It's easier to say who I am NOT. I am not "A Being", I am not "A God". I am not "A Divine Person", definitely not "A Trinity of Divine Persons." Talk about a schizoid personality! If being split in two is bad, how would you like to be split in Three? Is that a multiple personality syndrome or what: Trinophrenia?

"I am definitely not Allah. Not the Christian God of the Crusaders and George Bush!

'Onward Christian Soldiers' indeed! Anybody who makes God into a separate Being apart from the universe is an idolater."

"I immediately broke in, 'But that means that all of the believers in the monotheistic religions are idolaters. That means that all Muslims are infidels, all Jews are breaking the First Commandment, all Christians are infidels and idolaters, especially the ones who believe that Jesus Christ is God.'

"No, not all of them," She said, 'Only the fundamentalists, only the ones who take their scriptures as literal logos rather than myth.'

"'But almost all Jews, Muslims, and Christians believe God is a Divine Person, ' I said.

"'Then they are fundamentalists, infidels, and idolaters,' God answered. 'They need to read their scriptures. What I was inspiring their Scripture Writers to say was myth, metaphor, a manner of speaking that could not fully express unconscious being. You, my therapist, are an infidel and idolater if you really think I am a Divine Person talking to you right now as you write.'

"I assured Her that I did NOT think She was a Divine Person, but was the Ground of Being, or Ultimate Concern, somehow accessing my unconscious, and I loved her very much Whoever or Whatever She was.

"God was relieved to hear that I at least got that one right. But She still hadn't solved Her Identity Problem.

"'What else are you NOT?' I asked.

"'I am not Allah, the God of Holy War. There is no such thing as a Holy War. I am not the Allah who smiles on suicidal fanatics who slaughter my children mercilessly, viciously, and satanically. I am not George W. Bush's God of 'Infinite Justice', who slaughters more innocents, who really is the God of Vengeance, and a throwback to the Nazi God of 'Might Makes Right', in disguise.'

"At least God knows who She ISN'T. I can't wait for Her to tell us Who She IS."

As I finished this Chapter, I received an E-mail from Bob Woods one of the correspondents on our ex-Redemptorist list, complaining about the World War II Memorial in Washington, D.C. Bob was quite upset that in quoting President Roosevelt's Declaration of War on Japan, they left out the end of Roosevelt's Proclamation in which he asked God to help us destroy the Japanese Empire. Visitors to the Memorial are incensed because God was left out. So, We "the Greatest Generation" won that war against Japanese Imperialism and German/Italian Fascism, because the God, whom I just proved never existed, was on our side. No She wasn't.

Chapter II
The God Who Always Was

F ROM *THE DAY God Died*: "Now that we know who You are NOT, ARE You ready to tell us who You ARE?'

"Gladly, " She said, with a smile that broke as big as a rainbow after a dismal storm.

"I am the Primal Matter of the First Explosion. "I am the Thirteen Billion Year expanding universe.

"I am the Love Song of the Endless Spheres, the Gravity of the Galaxies, the Silence of the Cosmic Black Holes.

"I am the churning waters of the Primeval Sea, the Rivers Running from the louds, the Womb of Living Brine from which all life flows.

"I am the Endless Evolution marching from the Salty Sea. I am your Home which you left at birth, and the Home to which you shall return.

"I am the Center of the Circle of your Sojourn.

"I am Gaia, the Living Earth, and Cosmos, the Living Universe.

"I am Danaos, earth mother of the River Danube, goddess of fertility.

"I am Godde, the Soul of All Reality, the Anima of life itself.

"I am the Self Itself of the Universe.

"I am the Ground of Being, the Unconscious Being underlying All That Is.

"I am the All in All, the Only One, the Everything.

"I am Ultimate Concern, I am Love itself.

"I am all of the above and none of the above.'

"Now do you know who I am?"

Having, hopefully, established the fact that the God we all grew up with never really existed, what God DID exist, and who was this God? Now some will ask, "How do you prove God exists?" I answer, "You can't prove God exists! All you can do is prove that the various versions of God that we discussed in Chapter I never really existed."

Now, you ask, "How do I prove that these versions of God never existed?" I answer, "Because God told me! Read my book!" You answer, "Wait a minute. You just said that God never existed, and yet the only way you know that, is that this God who never existed told you he never existed?!?!"

Not exactly, what I meant was: my new version of God told me that your old version of God never existed. But MY version of God is alive and well and living in my unconscious, and this is the God who always was. But, you ask, isn't my version of God nothing but a figment of my own imagination? Perhaps, but I know that my version of God is just a metaphor, a symbol, floating on the surface of my unconscious, like an iceberg floating in the North Atlantic. There is just enough sticking up above the surface for my conscious mind to detect it. But like icebergs, 9/10ths of the contents are hidden from my conscious awareness.

Remember when we were taught sacramental theology? Even little kids who just reached the use of reason, who were still hovering on the cusp of the "Magic Years" when they could not distinguish fantasy from reality, could understand what the Sacrament of Christ's Body was about. They were told that Communion was an "outward sign, signifying a hidden reality." Somehow they knew Jesus Christ was in there somewhere even though, outwardly, it looked like a piece of bread. Without explaining the concept of symbolism to them, they understood the reality that something very sacred was going on.

In her "Case For God", Karen Armstrong, (Pg. 305) refutes the new atheists:

"The new atheists all equate faith with mindless credulity. Harris wrote "The End of Faith" immediately after 9/11, insisting that the only way to rid our world of terrorism was to abolish all faith. Like Dawkins and Hitchens, he defines faith as "Belief without Evidence," an attitude that he regards as morally reprehensible. It is not surprising, perhaps, that he should confuse "faith" with "belief" (meaning the intellectual acceptance of a proposition) because the two have become unfortunately fused in modern consciousness. But like other atheists and agnostics before him, Harris goes on to declare that faith is the root of all evil. A belief might seem innocent enough, but once you have blindly accepted the dogma that Jesus "can be eaten in the form of a cracker," you have made a space in your mind for other monstrous fictions: that God desires the destruction of Israel, the ethnic cleansing of Palestinians, or the 9/11 massacres. Everybody must stop believing in anything that cannot be verified by the empirical methods of science. It is not enough to get rid of extremists, fundamentalists, and terrorists. 'Moderate' believers are equally guilty of the 'inherently dangerous' crime of faith and must share responsibility for the terrorist atrocities."

I don't think you have to have a doctorate in Philosophy or Theology to see the silliness of the atheists' arguments against all faith and belief. How could they have never heard of metaphor and symbolism in religious faith and practice? How could they equate psychotic fanatics with well-mannered middle class Church goers? Harris and his atheist friends must be kidding or else profoundly ignorant of the difference between religious metaphor and scientific experimental facts? It is true that 78 years ago, when I received first communion, my mother told me not to bite and chew the host because that would of course be disrespectful, but not because I was eating Jesus' flesh! Even fourteen hundred years ago, St. Augustine of Hippo(North Africa), preached to his congregation that when they received communion and answered 'Amen' to 'The Body of Christ,' they were not assenting to a midget Jesus being present in bread, but were saying 'yes' to the mission to be in my world today, what Jesus was in his day: a witness to the Love of God in the world and the responsibility to love all my brothers and sisters in the human family. This is why, in the Ambrosian rite in Milan, Italy, you are not allowed to go to communion if you are at enmity with any of your neighbors. Of course, the above mentioned St. Augustine learned his Christianity from St. Ambrose in Milan.

When I was in Italy in November, 2004, and mentioned visiting Michelangelo's masterpiece in the Sistine Chapel, I ended up our trip in Milan, visiting my cousins there. On our last day in Italy, they took us to Mass, and I was struck by the difference in the Ambrosian rite. First of all, the Kiss of Peace and Reconciliation took place before the Canon of the Mass, not after it. And when time came for Communion, I missed going up to the altar because so few people went to communion. Perhaps most people in that Parish were not in a very forgiving mood that Sunday.

I hardly think the atheist cranks are familiar with all these nuances. But my personal problem is not with atheists, but with fundamentalist Catholics who insist on "transubstantiation," and are willing to die for the dogma that the "Bread and the Wine" are actually changed into the "Body and Blood" of Jesus Christ, and the "Sacrifice of the Mass" is actually a reenactment of the death of Jesus on the Cross where he died for our sins and opened up the gates of heaven, which had been closed since the original sin of Adam and Eve. The official Catholic Church still puts this idolatrous teaching in their catechisms without saying a word about it all being a myth and metaphor and symbolic ritual. What I am asking for along with many other "prophets" of the New Christianity in the New Millennium, is that we leave behind the literal interpretation of our Dogmas, and Creeds, and accept the metaphorical interpretation of them as they continue to evolve. That is the beauty of metaphor and symbol, it can always mean more than it did before, while literal, scientifically proven statements or authoritatively, infallibly decreed definitions are fixed in stone. A good example is the mystery of the Holy Trinity. For almost two thousand years, the dogma of the Trinity has remained the same. It is called a "De Fide" statement that must be believed under pain of mortal sin and eternal damnation. It isn't so much the mortal sin and damnation thing that bothers me, but the "defining" of the definition of the dogma. Define and definition both come from the same root: "finis": end, limit, border, fence. So once you define a teaching, you limit it completely, so that it can never mean any more or any less than the original literal meaning. Take the Nicene Creed, which at the Council of Nicea in 325 A.D. defined not only the Trinity, but all the basic teachings of the Church at the time. I find it quite ironic that there is no word in Italian for "Creed", but the Nicene Creed is referred to as "Il simbolo", from the Greek word: synbolein, meaning a "putting together" of various aspects of teachings. Symbol does not mean limiting by defining infallibly a literal truth, but symbol merely puts together various statements that symbolize, outwardly signify, mysteries that cannot be defined, but can continue to be explored until the end of limited, temporary human time. To simplify it for our purposes here, the Church teaches there is only One God, but there are three persons in God: the Father, the Son, and the Holy Spirit. Now the Son has two natures: Divine and human. The Son proceeds from the Father, and the Holy Spirit proceeds from the Father and the Son together. Just an aside, to point out the silliness of authoritarian dogma, the Orthodox Greek Christians split from the "Unorthodox" Roman Christians because the Orthodox (correct teaching) was that the Holy Spirit proceeded from the 2nd Person alone, while the (incorrect teaching) said that the Holy Spirit proceeded from Both the First Person and the Second Person. This was supposed to be part of the profound mystery of the Trinity. I doubt if anybody had any idea what proceeding from the Father and/or the Son could possibly mean.

Between you and me, it was no mystery that the intellectual Greeks had a profound hatred for their unintellectual and more aggressive Roman conquerors. As Colin Quinn the comedian, said recently, the Greeks were the greatest thinkers who ever lived, and the Romans were the greatest warriors, so the Romans sailed over the Aegean Sea and beat the crap out of the Greek thinkers and said "Now what do youse think about that?"

Okay, now what do you think about this? What if we take the Trinity as a metaphor for all of reality? What if we poetically muse that God the Father is a symbol of Being Itself, and Being Itself expresses itself through the evolution of matter. What if matter, the Word or Expression, of Being, becomes Being's way of knowing itself? Didn't Teilhard deChardin say that we were "Evolution conscious of itself?" What if we, human beings, as the only self—conscious beings that we are aware of in the universe, reveal Being to Itself? Then the so-called Second Person of the Trinity, the Word of God would be a metaphor for all of mankind! There is a beautiful translation of the Gospel of John that talks about: "In the beginning was the Word." J.B. Phillips, "The New Testament in Modern English, NY, Macmillan, 1962" translates John thus: "At the beginning God expressed Himself. That personal expression, that Word was with God and was God, and he existed with God from the beginning. All creation took place through him." What a beautiful, poetic way of saying that Jesus was the symbol of all of us as the Father's (Being's) expression of Himself.

I know that most believers and unbelievers alike will find this really farfetched, but give it a chance. Being itself in its bare concept does not have any consciousness in the sense that we humans understand consciousness, especially, sensuous consciousness, which is the only consciousness we can speak of. Now imagine Being-in-Itself evolving into visible matter, whether you call it creation or emanation, makes no difference, because we are only speaking metaphorically. Being, which is unconscious, i.e. has no self-awareness, no Ego, now is conscious of Itself through us? What if 'To know me is to love me', and Being loves itself because it now knows itself through creation? What if Being loves itself so much that it experiences ecstasy, jumps out of itself in bliss, something like the Big Bang, and gives off a Holy Spirit, the third Person of the Trinity? Just a metaphor, just a poem that keeps on giving. I have used it for my mantra in meditation daily for the past forty years. I learned this Sanskrit mantra back in the late 60's when Transcendental Meditation was in vogue, and they encouraged their disciples to use Sanskrit for their mantras because Sanskrit is older and closer to nature. So I took 'Sat-chit-ananda when I found out that it sounds like a Hindu Trinity. Sat means 'Being'= God the Father. Chit means 'Knowledge', the Word of God, or God the Son. Ananda means 'bliss,' the Spirit of Joy, of knowing and loving that you are. Satchitananda= in English: Being,

Knowledge, Love, and Bliss has provided me with thousands of hours of centering prayer in which I sink into the center of my existence and become one in the eternal NOW with the Oneness of All Being and the source of All Life.

Those of you who are still following this rambling description of God and me must certainly be wondering where I am going with all of this. In the first chapter I foolishly talked about the 'God who never was.' Now I have launched into a discussion of the God who always was, as if I know God on a first name basis. So here is my disclaimer:

I do not know WHAT God is; I do not know WHO God is; I don't even know THAT God is. I don't know why I am even talking about God. I spent the first 80 years of my life searching for God and asking questions about God because 'God' is the universal word used to refer to 'a higher power', 'the source of life', the 'Ground of Being', the 'Uncaused Cause', and we could go on for an hour with all the words and expressions used by humans down the years to refer to 'Ultimate Reality.' But I promised everyone in "The Day God Died" that the God we grew up with is alive and well and living in their home town, except that She is not exactly the same God we thought He was. Now I hope I have established once and for all that the God we all grew up with never existed, and I am engaged in the difficult pursuit of the God who always was. Just remember that I am using the word God in a very symbolic and metaphorical sense. As humans, we can never know if a God actually exists and if He does, what He might be. But in the metaphorical sense, the God who never existed was a 'Theistic" God. A theistic God is a God who is a separate being from the universe. He is not only a separate being in his own right, but he existed before the universe began, (presumably in the Big Bang of the astrophysicists, or the seven day Creationism of the biblical fundamentalists, or the intelligent design of other Creationists.) Believers in the theistic God, especially of the Abrahamic faiths: Judaism, Christianity, and Islam, believe their God actually intervened in history and chose special people to be His prophets, or even His Son. The theistic God is very personal and very human, and even though believers disclaim that he is nothing but an anthropomorphic projection, he is just that. Anthropomorphic means that humans can only think of other beings, whether creatures or creators, in human terms. The Greek philosopher, Xenophanes of Colophon, got into a lot of trouble making fun of the Greek Gods with all their human foibles by saying, "If horses could draw, they would draw their gods like horses." Of course when the monotheistic God was invented by Jews, Christians, and Muslims, they very clearly did not want a Greek, Roman, Hindu, or Valhalla God in their own image and likeness, but they created One nonetheless. Even though they claim the monotheistic God is pure spirit, they still have him acting throughout history as if he is a Big Overgrown Colossal Man. So if God is not this omnipotent, omniscient, supernatural Almighty Person, who is He?

I am usually 'accused' of being a pantheist when I talk like this. 'Accused' is the right expression because people say I just killed God by saying that everything is God. 'Pantheism' means that everything is God, and God is everything. Now when my accusers say this, they are using their definition of God as the almighty, all-knowing Supernatural One. Obviously, I am not that and you are not that, so what are they trying to prove? For forty years now, we progressives have been saying that 'pan-en-theism' is the correct expression, namely, that everything is IN God. Now, I am going back to the correct meaning of pantheism, meaning that God is, indeed everything, if God is understood as 'the ground of being', 'ultimate concern', or 'ultimate mystery.' We have to understand what the 'Oneness of Being' is about.

Many Greek Philosophers taught that 'All Being is One". They also taught that 'All Being is True', 'All Being is Good', and 'All being is beautiful'. They called this 'monism' while others preferred 'dualism', which was all about the division of reality into natural vs. supernatural, material vs. spiritual, mind vs' matter, and so on. In the past two thousand years, we have been schooled in a world of dualism, and that is why there has been an absolute separation between God and us. God has been the 'sacred other' from us, and like East and West, 'never the twain shall meet.' Lately, in the new millennium, various movements have arisen both in the east and in the west espousing this Oneness of Being. The Sufi sect of Islam has long espoused the teaching from the Quran of the Oneness of Being. They are famous for their 'Whirling

Dervishes' who are practitioners of God as Oneness containing us all, and their whirling dance is a way of centering oneself in the depth of the Oneness. They have recently made popular all over the world the 'Dances of Universal Peace' in which groups hold hands and dance in a circle to express their Oneness of Being. Many progressive Christians have adopted the circle as a better representation of brotherly love than the pyramid with the Pope on top and the hierarchy below him, and then the clergy, and finally the people, as the 'subjects' of the higher ups. Most are unaware, of course, of the new trend toward seeing us all as One in a Ground of Being called Love. But we are working on it very slowly. A new book that came out in 2004, called "This Is It", by Jan Kersschott, a Belgian practitioner of natural medicine, makes the case for Oneness of Being, or Unicity. He writes that there is not only One Being in the Universe that includes all being, but there is actually only *BEINGNESS*. This is his ultimate barrage against non-duality. There isn't even One Being, but only Beingness! There is absolutely no separateness anywhere in which to hide. (*THIS IS IT:The Nature of Oneness*, by Jan Kersschot, Watkins Pubishing, London 2004.)

Let me conclude this chapter on the 'God Who Always Was' by quoting the second book of this Trilogy, The Day My Ego Died, pg.177. I was mourning the fact that I had to give up my Ego, and my imagined, metaphorical God says, " I had to give up my Ego a long time ago. In fact, I never had an Ego. I was content to let all of you name me. And most of you did a terrible job of identifying Me.

"I don't care at all for the Judeo-Christian Bible's description of Me. You make me too distant, too awesome, too judgmental, too punishing. And the Muslim idea of Me as Allah is very unappealing, aloof, even embarrassing. At least the rest of the religions leave me alone, ignore me, or just worship their ancestors instead of me."

"I could tell that God was depressed at the terrible image the monotheists of the world had projected on Her throughout the centuries. So I repeated to her the paean I had given her at the end of her therapy sessions with me:

"You are the joy of making love, the bubble of a baby's smile.

"You are the tear in the toddler's eye, the prettiness of the puppy.

"You are the silence of the slave, weeping to be freed, the gall of the oppressed struggling to survive.

"You are the compassion for the poor, the strength of the meek.

"You are the hope of those who wait, the security of those who believe.

"You are the freedom of the prisoner, the forgiveness of the condemned.

"You are the loveliness of the leaf, the green in the billowing grass.

"You are the fragrance of the flower, the shelter of the trees.

"You are the broadness of the plains, the snow-covered awe of mountains.

"You are the azure sky, and sun-filled clouds. "You are the aquamarine waters of the oceans, the sweep of the continents.

"You are the Holder of the Globe, hurler of the Moon, the Infinite power of sunstars, and the breathtaking awe of planets and their satellites. "You are the gravity of the galaxies, the force of the universe, the Strider of the Milky Way, The Fourth of July explosions of nebulae. You are the One, the True, the Good, and the Beautiful. You are the Ground of All Being. You are Ultimate Concern.

"You are Love."

CHAPTER III
WHAT ABOUT ME?

From *The Day My Ego Died*, **pp.175**

" I SENSED THAT GOD was through with my therapy, and was trying to ease my separation-anxiety which occurs at the end of every course of treatment."

"'I need you,' I said, 'to help me say goodbye to my Ego.' And I became more than somewhat weepy."

"'You know, I poured a lot of pain and suffering into this Ego. It suffered guilt, loss, terror, and depression.'

"'Then you should be glad to get rid of it!' "'But I invested so much time and energy into my ego, so much anxiety and sleepless nights. So many 'Examinations of Conscience', kept so many rules and regulations. Even though I broke many, I kept even more. I worked so hard to get people to accept me, to like me, even, God forbid, love me. All for the exaltation of my miserable FUCKING EGO! I began very softly, I might say *pianissimo*, then gradually went through *piano*, until I reached *forte* and then *fortissimo*, and when I shouted the 'f' word, I was in full *crescendo*.

"'You know you only use that word when you are angry,' God said. ' What are you so mad about?

"'All the wasted years! My life was a fucking Ego trip! It benefited absolutely no one, especially myself!

"God was not that sympathetic. ' You have never been able to separate well. Every time you have to say goodbye to someone, you always manage to say something stupid, something hurtful, so they will be glad to let you go, and you won't miss them. You have had some truly miserable break-ups.

"'But this time, it being the time I get to see my Ego, I really am sorry to let it go.'

"Of course you are. So why do your usual 'I hate you, I never liked you, routine? ' Why pretend that your life was a stupid waste, so you can let it go easier? Remember Kuhbler—Ross's second stage of death is anger, and you are deep into it now.

"My hurt was too great to really say it. ' I am very lazy, and I can't bear to think that I worked so much harder than I needed to. Maybe there is something I can salvage from my Ego trip. I am such a pack rat, there must be something I can keep out of a lifetime of Ego work!

"Let it all go, and get into your depression and loss funk, God said.

"It feels so much like losing my self. How can I let go of my self? Remember that play, *A Thousand Clowns?* It was about identity. The uncle who had custody of his nephew wanted him to know why he was born a man and not a chair! I worked my ass off all my life, to find out who I was as opposed to everyone else. And now you are asking me to throw my unique identity into the garbage. You want me to become one other brick in a building full of billions of bricks?

"That's right. I want you all to be identical. I made you all unique. It was your job to become identical."

"'Now that is really depressing!', I said.

"'Ah feel yo' pain!' she did her Bill Clinton again. ' I had to give up my Ego a long time ago. In fact, I never had an Ego. I was content to let all of you name me. And most of you did a terrible job of identifying me!'

What about me? If God is not an individual person, why do I insist on being an individual person? Many will say that the concept

of a personal God is just a projection of egocentric humans who think they are unique human persons. In conversations and discussions over the past ten years, I have found that most people, especially observant Catholics, have a hard time accepting the fact that God is not a person like us. After all we were taught so consistently throughout the first two millennia that God is an omnipotent, and omniscient entity (read *person*, the only way we humans can describe a knowing and powerful being). We were taught by the self-proclaimed "infallible magisterium" of the hierarchy that God personally intervened in history, sent his only begotten Son down from heaven to die for our sins and open up the gates of heaven (which happened to be closed since Adam and Eve got kicked out of the Garden of Eden, after they committed "Original Sin") You know the rest of the story, you were told so many times.

How can I get most Christians to accept the self evident truth that God is not a person, never mind *THREE* PERSONS? And because they have this problem with the personality of God, they have a bigger, closer to home, problem with their own personhood.

When people read *The Day My Ego Died* they rejected the idea that they needed to kill their own Ego's. Just as most people could not understand that we humans have created God in our own image and likeness, they cannot understand that we have created our individual Ego's with the same anthropomorphic projections with which we created a personal God.

Certainly, Freud would agree wholeheartedly that the typical religious person projects (read,) *makes up* his own God, but I doubt if he would agree that we also project, that is, make up our own personal Ego. After all, Freud is famous for stating that there was no Almighty 'Father in Heaven' Person, and that he, Freud, was the true Messiah for whom the Jews had been waiting for about 5,701 years. That took quite a large manufactured Ego on Freud's part (not to mention chutzpah). We are fond of saying "You just can't make this stuff up." But in Freud's case he has turned this street proverb on its head and made up something about his Ego that trumps what the Christians were saying about Jesus Christ for two millennia.

So if somebody as important as God turns out to be a nobody (in the sense that I explained in Chapters I and II,) what happens to our Ego? Are we a somebody or a nobody?

The next three chapters will attempt to explain the *Birth of Ego*, the *Death of Ego*, and lastly the process of *Dying To Ego* which I call the *Dark Night of the Ego*.

CHAPTER IV
THE BIRTH OF EGO

FROM *THE BOOK of Tao* (pronounced 'dhow',) "There is something mysterious, without beginning, without end, that existed before the heaven and earth. Unmoving, infinite; standing alone; never changing. It is everywhere and it is inexhaustible. It is the mother of all.

"I do not know its name. If I must name it I call it Tao ('The Way') and I hail it as supreme. Looked for it cannot be seen; it is invisible. Listened for it cannot be heard; it is inaudible. Reached for it cannot be touched; it is intangible. These three are beyond analysis; these three are one.

"The scholar needs to know more and more each day. The follower of Tao needs to know less and less each day. By lessening knowledge one reaches inaction. By inaction everything can be done. The world is won by those who leave it alone. When one feels compelled to dominate, the world is already beyond reach."

(Can you imagine Jesus, the Jewish peasant, hearing these words from Lao Tzu?)

"The heavens endure,; the earth is very old. Why? Because they do not exist for themselves, they therefore have long life.

"The truly wise are content to be last; they are therefore first. They are indifferent to themselves; they are therefore self-confident. Perhaps it is because they do not exist for themselves that they find complete fulfillment.

"Thus, the truly wise seek Unity, they embrace oneness, and become examples for all the world. Not revealing themselves, they shine; not self-righteous, they are distinguished; not self-centered, they are famous; not seeking glory, they are leaders.

"Because they are not quarrelsome, no one quarrels with them. Thus it is as the ancients said: 'To yield is to retain Unity.' The truly wise have Unity, and the world respects them.

(From *The Book of Tao*, Peter Pauper Press, Mt. Vernon, NY 1962)

Before we proceed any further, we should look to Lao Tzu, the ancient Chinese philosopher, for his perspective on ultimate reality which he calls the 'Tao', now called 'Dao', and I assure you it is quite the opposite of the Dow-Jones. When I was making my case for the death of Ego, I found this quote from the delightful Book of Tao which so clearly states that there is no room in human existence for what we westerners so proudly hail as our big, fat free Ego's. "The truly wise are content to be last; they are therefore first." Doesn't that sound like Jesus' "Last shall be first and first shall be last?" How about, "The meek shall inherit the earth?", and "Happy the poor, because God's Kingdom here on earth really belongs to them?"

So what about ME and my Ego? Most westerners who have been brought up on Ego psychology have no idea what I am talking about, so I need to discuss: *The Birth of Ego.* Especially the Baby Boomers of the U.S.A., who were fed heavy doses of self-esteem for breakfast, lunch and dinner, so much so that they became the "Me Generation" after the "Great Generation" of WWII fame bequeathed them the most prosperous economy the world has ever seen. Of course, the military-industrial complex of America along with their neo-Imperialists eventually bankrupted the entire world's economy because of their unbridled greed and Ego. During these last ten years since 9/11/01 I have often laughed at how this world wide disaster was all scapegoated on a small bunch of Muslim Jihadi's.

I am now consolidating my thoughts and feelings about the rise of Ego. At the National Catholic School of Social Services (CUA) in

Washington, D.C., I was taught Ego Psychology which is another name for Neo-Freudian analysis. After two years of intense practice under supervision, and many post graduate courses in analysis using the latest learning's in Ego Psychology, I made some progress in understanding my own neuroses along with the neuroses and psychoses of my patients. But no one ever told me that Ego was an invention of psychologists and psychiatrists, under the leadership of Sigmund Freud, to make some sense out of the infinite craziness of the human psyche. Not that they really invented Ego, but they gave a name to that product of the human brain that was developed over thousands of years of evolution through the "survival of the fittest" processes of natural selection. Does Ego exist as a 'being' in its own right? Of course not. Ego is a mental construct of the reptilian brain, that acts as some kind of CEO of the human being, just to get it to survive as long as possible without being consumed or used as a stepping stone by other human beings. The Ego is a false self, a survival mechanism of the human animal. Just as Ego psychology creates an elaborate system of "Mechanisms of Defense" of the Ego, so the Ego itself is a mechanism of defense for the survival of the individual. But nobody ever tells you that your Ego is not really you at all but a false self posing as the real you. The real you is the spirit self, made, as traditional Judeo-Christian theology says, in the image and likeness of God who is pure spirit.

I am fond of saying that Carl Jung was one of the first to reject Ego as defined by the Freudians. He referred to God as the *SELF* with a capital 'S', and each human as a self with a low case 's'. But we need to talk more about Ego as we westerners were taught. One of the best books on the subject of Ego psychology is Erik Erikson's *Childhood and Society*, (1950, W.W.Norton, New York). In it, Erikson talked about the 8 stages of Ego development through 8 crises. The first stage takes place during the first two years of development, which he calls: *Trust versus Mistrust*. The first crisis we have is whether to trust this world into which we have been violently thrust, or we are doomed to mistrust others and life itself for the rest of our lives. This is where paranoia, the deadliest of mental illnesses comes from. Sigmund Freud had graphically described the birth process as a violent and traumatic act of aggression in which the birthing fetus is thrust out of the womb after 9 months of tranquil dependency. Freud said that no one really is ready for birth, but we are violently expelled from the nest into a hostile world where you are on your own after a gestation of unconscious paradise. You have no idea that you are a separate being from your mother, but think you are fused with her.

In the first stage of *Trust versus mistrust*, the infant emerges from its uterine omnipotence to gradually sense that it is powerless and totally dependent on the surrounding caretakers and must learn to trust them or be doomed to a paranoid existence of fear and anxiety. If we learn to trust, we can learn to get up off our bellies and walk and become toddlers who trust their parents enough to say 'NO' which is the only way they have of stating that they are individuals separate from their parents. Thus the Birth of Ego. Prior to the birth of Ego, which is the consciousness of our individuality, that is, our separateness from other people, we are fused with our mothers. As I said above, we have a delusional infantile omnipotence in which we think that we ARE the world, or rather that the whole world exists for us. This is not the *Trust versus Mistrust* crisis that Erikson refers to, but rather the first attempts at an awareness of our individuality. Interestingly enough, our essential spiritual natures are born with the spiritual, unconscious sense that we are one with the universe, but our evolutionary genes take over and drive us into separateness and individuality. Erikson talked constantly about identity and was really defined by his work on Identity and Youth. The whole purpose of Ego Psychology according to him was identity, individuation, and separateness, uniqueness from everyone else. It is very poignant that it was later revealed that Erikson secretly knew, or thought he knew, that he was the illegitimate son of the King of Denmark, and suffered all his life because he was never acknowledged by his father. That is identity with a big bang behind it.

But now I want to return to the roots of identity. The Latin word "idens" from which comes "identity" really means "the same," that is, "Oneness with All." I quoted above that God said in *the Day My Ego Died* that he made us all unique and its our job to become identical with the oneness of being. I now revise that and say that evolution made each of us human beings unique, but it is the task of spirituality to make us all identical. I again go to *The Day My Ego Died*: "God answered in a deep meditation, 'Don't be so hung up on who you are, as opposed to everyone and everything else in the universe.

Besides, *who* you are, and *what* you are, are two entirely different concepts.'

"'Say what?' I asked in my best Ebonics. "'Who you are refers to your Ego as a separate center of consciousness. It is a combination of millions of years of genetic inheritance combined with your own lifetime of decisions for better and for worse. To that conglomerate of genes, and decisions, we give a name: Sal Umana. But essentially this unique *You* is a figment of your own imagination.'

"'But didn't we sing in the Marriage Encounter Movement, 'Yes, I know I'll never find another you.'

(Yes, but we also sang another song," If you can't be with the one you love, then love the one you're with.)

"'Oh, that's a lovely romantic idea that's been foisted on you by this adolescent pop culture, begging for esteem, whining immaturely to know your unique identity.'

"' But,' I said, 'look at all the cemeteries and burial places that go back through the pyramids to the very beginning of 'homo sapiens'.

"Yes, ' God admitted, 'Mankind has always yearned for immortality and has always wanted to keep his own unique identity forever, but look at *Me*, do I wonder about *My* identity? Do I care *Who* I am? It's not an accident that no one has ever discovered the identity of God. Nobody ever has, and nobody ever will, because I don't know who I am either. So why do you care who *You* are?

"' Now *What* you are—that is a different story. What I am, what you are, what the universe is, *THAT* is what matters. That is the only identity that you should care about. 'You are a child of the universe' as *Desiderata* says. You are, as Teilhard DeChardin says, 'Evolution conscious of itself'. That's what you are!'

"'And what are you?', I asked Her.

"'I am the Ground of All Being. I am the Universe. I am evolution itself.'

"'And you are my voice."

"'If that is the truth about me', I said, 'Then it should set me free."

"' And if it doesn't set you free, it is not the truth.'

"Like St.Exupyree's *Little Prince*, I repeated, 'And if it doesn't set me free, it is not the truth.'

Chapter V
The Death of Ego

From Ekhart Tolle, *A New Earth: Awakening To Your Life's Purpose (Penguin Group, NY,NY 2005)*

"For thousands of years, humanity has been increasingly mind-possessed, failing to recognize the possessing entity as 'not self.' Through complete identification with the mind, a false sense of self—the Ego—came into existence. The density of the Ego depends on the degree to which you – the consciousness—are identified with your mind, with thinking. Thinking is no more than a tiny aspect of the totality of consciousness, the totality of who you are." P. 130

"Emotions and the Ego"

"The Ego is not only the unobserved mind, the voice in the head which pretends to be you, but also the unobserved emotions that are the body's reaction to what the voice in the head is saying." P. 134

I am very grateful to Ekhart Tolle for clarifying so many concepts that were racing abstractedly through my mind in the aftermath of 9/11 and the self-analysis of my two books. Tolle expounded all these new and some not so new ideas about divinity and the human Ego. Just to name some of the Chapters: Ego: The Current State of Humanity; Role-Playing: The Many Faces of Ego; Finding Who You Truly Are. It goes without saying that I recommend you immediately find yourself a copy of his books.

I have tried to explain something of the Birth of Ego, and the necessity of understanding what Ego is in terms of psychotherapy and analysis. Now its time to talk about the Death of Ego. Back in the late 70's, when I was learning how to be a psychotherapist at the Catholic University of America, we were given a lecture by the Hemlock Society which originated in Washington, DC. The Hemlock Society, as far as I know, were the first ones to promote assisted dying. They never used the words "assisted suicide", because they wanted to avoid all the religious, legal, emotional, and moral problems associated with suicide. Quite obviously, they were not able to avoid the latter, but they carried on in privacy with as much secrecy as they could. Their whole message in lecturing us was the courage involved in gathering a group together who would meet regularly and discuss all the implications of what they were doing.

Above all it was a spiritually sharing group, who meditated and prayed together at length. When the time came for the person in question to die, the group met in a religious service, or spiritual service, whatever they had decided to do as a group, and assisted the Socrates in question to 'shuffle off his mortal coil' whether by quaffing hemlock or whatever was the drug of choice. Above all, it was a beautiful experience for all present. We hope it was as beautiful for the designated dier, or diehard. (I am not sure what word to use here.)

But we are talking here about the death of the Ego, not the death of the body. The death of the body as advocated by the Hemlock Society should take place in groups. Don't try this on your own at home. I also advise that when it comes to the Death of Ego, we should not try it alone at home. We need the help of a group, whether a therapy group, a prayer group, a worship group, a zen group. We need to be surrounded by others who can help us see through our Ego= false-self. Obviously, they must be people who share the values and insights of this book and the authors quoted. For now, we have to talk about the Death of Ego.

In Chapter II of this book, The God Who Always Was, I pointed out that we know very little about God, and most of what we know is what God is *NOT*. We found out that God is not a big person, with a Big Ego, and a free will, and an all-knowing Mind. God is not even *A* being. But God is something we humans invented as a way of understanding our own transcendence. Now this is an uncanny ability that we humans have of inventing artificial personalities whether it is in God or in ourselves or in any living flora or fauna, even in rivers or mountains, or the earth itself, e.g. *Gaia* the Greek god signifying the Earth personified. For thousands of years, since the dawn of human self-consciousness, we humans have experienced the supernatural, the preternatural, the miraculous, the awesome and terrifying powers of nature, and have built up a vast lore of shared experiences that have no scientific or common sense explanation. So we tend to personify these unknown powers as gods, Great Spirits, Creators. Many religions have institutionalized their version of God, and spun out various theologies to explain their version of God, and our relationship with Him. (Most of the time, He is masculine, at least for the past three thousand years. I understand that prior to that, God or Godde (female form of God) was in the ascendancy, naturally, given the human tendency to look to our mothers as the source of life.) But it is very clear that the human tendency to personalize everything applies especially to the unknown or unmanifested powers in the universe.

Most versions of God in institutionalized religions are of God as a separate being. We modern progressives who are inclined towards spirituality as opposed to religious worship, reject the idea of God as a separate being from us and experience God as the transcendent aspect of our own being and becoming. In other words, we experience *God* as intimately part of ourselves, and conversely, ourselves as intimately part of God. Jesus expressed this as " I and the Father are One". Actually, we have no idea whether the historical Jesus actually said this, or what he might have meant if he actually said it. But most Biblical Scholars today would say that the writer of St.John's Gospel, which was written 60 or 70 years after the death of Jesus, had a mystical experience of Oneness with God, and wrote about it as if he were the resurrected Jesus Christ speaking metaphorically of our intimate relationship with God. It now seems that the first followers of Jesus, the Christ, *the anointed One of God,* believed that they were the Resurrected Body of Christ, all of them together as a community of faith which they called *The mystical body of Christ.* Thus they felt free to believe that what they were experiencing was the spirit of the risen Jesus in them as a community. Somehow, the man who had been crucified by the Romans was still accessible to them in a way so real and vivid that they talked about him as having *risen from the dead*. And since they knew intuitively that Jesus had been born again somehow in them, they were obliged to think and act like him. As St. Paul said, " Let this mind be in you which was also in Christ Jesus."

Now the ultimate question, of course, is, if we are all One in God, what about our uniqueness and individuality? Haven't we been told all our lives that we have to find out what is so special and unique about each one of us, like snowflakes, or finger prints? That is why, in the aftermath of *The Day God Died,* I struggled to analyze myself in *The Day My Ego Died.* The thesis of the book was that if God never was a person, how can I be a person? If God never had an Ego, what are we humans doing with Ego's? The essence of my agony in that book was not so much my need to know who I was, my true identity, but how to deal with what I am not. I found a God who was a nobody, a non-person, and inevitably, so was I a nobody, and a non-person. That is what I mean by the Death of Ego.

From the First Session of *The Day My Ego Died*:

"I turned to what was left of my idea of God and asked her to take me on as a patient.

'Why are you coming to *ME*?' she asked. 'Didn't you just write a book proving that I'm dead?'

'No I didn't! I just said that the God of theism is dead!'

'The God of theism is who I used to be?" 'No, not exactly,' I said. ' The God of theism is really a very primitive idea of God that goes back to the tribal gods of the Middle East, and to Greek, Roman, and Teutonic mythology.'

'So who am I?', God asked querulously.

'I told you in your therapy sessions with me! You are not a separate Supreme Being, rather, you are the Ground of All Being!'

'So I'm not a separate person in my own right? I'm not even a 'Multiple Personality Disorder' like the Father, Son, and Holy Spirit, three persons in One?'

'No to the first question, no to the second, and no to the third, ' I answered.

'Then why are you talking to me if I am not a person?'

'I am talking to whoever, or whatever You are,' I said, wondering if I was losing my mind.

'What in heaven or hell is that supposed to mean? Are you trying to say that you are talking to yourself and listening to yourself? All at the exact same time?'

'Bear with me awhile!' (Again the shouting.) 'This is just a literary device, in which the writer expresses his thoughts by inventing an imaginary character to talk to and listen to!'

'Beautiful! A real person would know that anyone who talks to himself is whacko!'

She wasn't going to make this easy for me. Perhaps I had come down too hard on the *Death of God* theme and now She was getting back at me.

'I already told you that you *are not dead, just the God of Monotheism is dead!* You still exist but I need to work on a new understanding of who or what you are!'

'Okay, let me see if I have this straight. I am what's left of your idea of God, after the God of monotheism died.'

'Something like that, but I don't know what to do with whatever God now is.'

'So, instead of the old all-powerful *guy in the sky with the pie,* I have become a *literary construct?*

'Just for the purpose of these therapy sessions! I have some new ideas of who you are: like You are the transcendent aspect of reality. You are the divine aspect of myself.'

'You got to be kidding! Now God has become a part of YOU?'

'I know that sounds crazy, but that seems to be the choice that God made God gives us dominion over Himself, or rather God signifies that He is part of our Self, and we are part of His Self.'

'I must be a very crazy God to do that. What you are saying is that I need you to know who I am.'

'What I am saying is that I believe you have chosen to do precisely that. You, God, have chosen to need me."

This passage was inspired by one of my favorite spiritual poets, Rainer Maria Rilke(*Rilke's Book of Hours: Love Poems to God*, translated by Anita Barrows and Joanna Macy: Riverhead Books, 1996, NY, NY.) I *quote* him in the Epigraph of *The Day God Died*:

'What will you do, God, when I die? 'I am your pitcher (when I shatter?)

'I am your drink (when I go bitter?) 'I, your garment; I your craft,

'Without me, what reason have you? 'What will you do, God? I am afraid.'

I doubt if Rainer Maria Rilke, when he wrote those words, had any idea about the Death of Ego, which brings me to my theory about intuition which I like to think is very intuitive. At the serious risk of seeming elitist, we intuitives already know (intuitively, of course) everything we will ever know, and when we see something 'new', or hear something 'new', it is really 'de'ja' vue' all over again for us. Which brings me to my theory about spiritual knowledge. The spirit already knows everything that it ever will know, because the spirit makes no progress, but already *IS*, as it was in the beginning, is now, and ever shall be, (as the ancient prayer says.) In fact there is only One Spirit, because Spirit is not a thing that can be divided into parts. The One Spirit includes you, and me, and all of us, and is the basis for the Oneness of Being.

Now how do we bridge the gap between spiritual, intuitive knowledge, and the self-conscious human brain? Poets and mystics like Rilke do it for a living. I am pretty sure that Rilke meant that God needed us to be his consciousness on earth. Just as that other great mystic, Teilhard DeChardin, could simply say that we humans are *Evolution Conscious of Itself*. But now I am pondering what happens to God, but especially to us, when our Ego dies. Without Ego, God has a greater presence in our spirit, our mindless, unconscious spirit. But what about us? What about me? What happens to me when my Ego dies?

One of my supervisors once said that all therapy was about separation and death. Each session we learn more about separation, and especially the final session of any course of therapy. We have to accept the bittersweet reality that we must say goodbye to someone we have grown to be comfortable with, and dependent on. This is especially true of our Ego. Even though it was a false-self that caused us grief, and anxiety, and pain, we had become dependent on it for some kind of identity and belonging, so precious to social animals like ourselves. My seventeen sessions of dying to Ego were like Jesus' agony in the Garden. "Dear God, don't let me die." But I could not say, "Not my will, but Thy Will be done," because it was *NOT* God's will that my Ego should die. God never had a will. That's a human faculty. God never had an Ego to lose. It was *MY* Ego to lose, and if God, the Ground of All Being, never had an Ego, how could I pretend to have an Ego, a center of attention, hubris, vanity, and "self-worth." The only worth my self ever had was to be part of the whole. "No man is an island, no man stands alone. Ask not for whom the bell tolls, it tolls for thee."

Was I finally at the funeral of my Ego? And was that bell a distant dream like the star I always wanted to be named after me, like the little St. Therese of Lisieux, who saw the 'T' in the sky (Orion's sword belt and sword) and told her father that God had put her initial in the sky. No, the Cosmic Papa will never put a big "S" in the sky for Sal. As I joke to my golf-mates, the big "S" I draw on my golfballs stands for big "Assa", in my father Chaahley's Boston-Italian accent.

CHAPTER VI
THE DARK NIGHT OF THE EGO

In "THE DAY My Ego Died," I did a heart-hurting, soul wrenching self-analysis springing from my newly confirmed analysis of God as unselfconscious Being. I agonized through 17 sessions of self-analysis, often weeping at the prospect that I had to give up my Ego. I didn't know it at the time, but I was going through the Dark Night of the Ego. In the novitiate, sixty years ago, we studied all about the "Dark Night of the Senses", and the "Dark Night of the Soul." I was fascinated by the lives of the medieval mystic St. Teresa of Avila and her tortured friend, St. John of the Cross, who in their wonderful Carmelite tradition wrote about the Dark Night of the Senses, which is very much like modern day depression, or better, as we psychotherapists now call it, *ANHEDONIA*, which is a total loss of sensual pleasure or even feeling of any kind, even negative feelings. But the dreaded Dark Night of the Soul was a total absence of the Presence of God. Interestingly enough, a biographer of Teresa of Calcutta recently revealed that his subject suffered the Dark Night of the Soul so severely that she doubted the existence of God for the last forty years of her life. Frankly, I think that Teresa of Calcutta simply suffered from the subconscious realization that the God of Theism: a special Supreme Person with a personal love for us as if it were a human personal love only infinitely better, never really existed. But, because of the religious culture of the Roman Catholic Church, especially of its conservative leader, the Pope, she was unable to accept the new ideas about God as Ultimate Concern, Ground of Being, and Love In Practice. But notice, Teresa DID GOD, that is, she acted out this new God, defined as Love Eternal, in her own life, even though she did not GET IT, intellectually. My guess is that Teresa of Calcutta GOT

IT intuitively, but was stuck with the traditional Catholic spirituality which she was taught in formation.

As for me, I had gone through the Dark Night of the Soul in my mid-life crisis when I was going through the agony of leaving the Priesthood, and I realized that the "Our Father Who Art in Heaven God" that I had prayed to all my life never really existed. So if Tillich's "Cosmic Papa" never existed, what about Sal Umana who based his whole life on Him? Did I really exist anymore as an individual? And if I and my Ego are the same thing, who am I, what am I? If God no longer exists as a separate being from the universe, how can I exist as a separate being from the universe? If the Ground of All Being is not an individual, how can I be? This is what I mean by the "Dark Night of the Soul."

Why does my Ego demand to be me, an individual being, separate from the universe? How can I be a separate being from the universe if God, the Ground of all being, cannot be a separate being from the universe? The Ground of All Being is not separate from the universe, it *IS* the universe. And if I come from the Ground of All Being, then I am one with All Being, not a separate individual.

Could moral evil be simply an insistence by the individual Ego on being separate? Maybe that is what sin is, what moral evil is: a refusal to be One with the Oneness of Being. Is this what the ancient teaching about "Original Sin" is trying to say? Our Judeo-Christian creation story has Adam and Eve committing the first sin by eating from the tree of the knowledge of good and evil. Could this be a metaphor for refusing to be our brother or sister, for lashing out to be different from everybody else, better, brighter, happier? I have told so many people, so many times to stop looking for God, to stop looking for happiness and success, and to pause and let God and happiness and success find them. Way back in the 70's Matthew Fox wrote a book entitled "Original Blessing", in which he said that there was no original sin, but original blessing, that by being born human we already had happiness and success, that we didn't need salvation, because we were already saved by being born human.

A friend and poet, John Chuchman, states this beautifully in a poem he sent us:

"The *Real* Good News we should be spreading is that."

We do not need to be *Saved* **from anything** other than a belief that we are solely human.

We were already *Saved* when we were born, saved from nothingness.

That is the Only *Salvation* **We will ever need,**

So how do we deal with Ego? Does Ego belong to the body or to the soul? It would seem that Ego is a construct of the material brain, and therefore, part of the body. Ego is the center of material consciousness, and of course, of self-consciousness. When the body dies, Ego dies with it, and thus self-consciousness as we know it now. But spiritual awareness, unconscious awareness, is a totally different concept. We know we have spiritual awareness now because when we engage in intuitive contemplation without any words or concepts, and cleanse our minds from all thoughts, our conscious brain knows that something in us is experiencing an inner, unconscious awareness. But there is no way of bringing the unconscious awareness to the surface of consciousness. There are no words to signify what the soul is experiencing unconsciously, immaterially, except some kind of metaphorical or symbolic expression in our material consciousness that attempts to convey an intimation of what went on in the cloud of unknowing.

Now volumes have been written about the conscious, the unconscious, the preconscious, and the subconscious. It is way beyond my competence to explain them to you. Freud, Jung, Adler, and Piaget, the big four of modern Ego Psychology talk about consciousness as it applies to their views of the human person. I only know that the consciousness and unconsciousness they talked about, dies with the body. I am talking about an awareness that is spiritual, immaterial, and eternal. There is no Rosetta stone for translating this unconscious awareness into self-conscious awareness.

The anonymous author of the medieval English study of mysticism: *THE CLOUD OF UNKNOWING*, writes about giving up conscious knowing and going into the cloud of not knowing, especially when it says in Chapter 43 that a "Soul is to destroy all knowing and feeling of its own being." (The Cloud of Unknowing: Introductory commentary and translation by Ira Progoff, NY, Julian Press, 1957.)

PROGOFF WRITES IN HIS INTRODUCTION:

"What the author of *The Cloud of Unknowing* seeks is thus not an experience or feeling of unity with God; but rather the establishment of a fact of existence, a condition of life, in which the individual is God-and vice-versa—in actuality, even if only for the briefest atom of a moment. "At such time, having overcome his attachments to the objects of life, the memory of past experiences and present desires, the memory and attachment to sacred figures and traditional observances, having overcome all these and whatever other thoughts of any kind may press upon the cloud of unknowing, a man comes very close to the naked being of human nature. And there, at that deepest ground of his being, he is no longer an individual as such, but he participates in the naked being that is God's ultimate nature. Then oneness becomes indeed a fact of his existence; and he can say with Meister Eckhart, "the eye with which I see God is the same with which God sees me."

As I write this, I find myself back in my novitiate, St. Mary's College, Ilchester, MD, 15 miles from Baltimore. It is sixty years ago, and I am locked into unconscious meditation. I am lost in "The Cloud of Unknowing". Ira Progoff tells me "if the individual feels or experiences himself as being in unity with God, that very feeling and awareness of an experience indicates that real unity has not yet been achieved. At such times, the author of *The Cloud of Unknowing* tells us, "If you look truly you will find" that something is still "between you and your God" (IX:1)There is still work remaining to be done." I would like to say that I emerged from mystical contemplation without an Ego, with no sense of separation from God, the Universe, the Oneness of Being. But my Ego is still here, alive and well and living and carousing in Freeport, Long Island. It seems that the Dark Night of the Ego is a spiritual agony that will go on till the death of my body.

I signed each copy of The Day My Ego Died: "You are already dead and living in heaven, in God's Eternal Now, but you will not enjoy it completely until all of your Ego is dead." I have to say that the last nine years of my life since I wrote that book have been the happiest of my 82 years. But my Ego is definitely not dead yet, so I need to commit to a lifestyle of Living Without Ego, and Dying Without Ego, so I can finally shuffle off this mortal coil and enter into the next level of awareness.

Chapter VII
Living Without Ego

As long as we are living in the flesh, we never really "come out" of the "Dark Night of the Ego." Many of us have experienced that the Dark Night of the Senses, (Depression/Anhedonia) comes and goes, whether for psychological reasons or for spiritual reasons. The same is true of the Dark Night of the Soul. Spiritual desolation alternates with spiritual consolation. Contemplative literature is full of instances of both, just as is the alternating suffering and joy of Zen.

Does the Dark Night of the Ego come and go? Of course! We never finally bury our Ego until it is placed in the coffin with our hands folded around it's neck in a throttling position. Before that, hopefully, happy day, we have to kill our Ego every time it rears its ugly head so we can enter each moment into the awakened state of Eternal Now. (The NOW, the awakened state, or Buddha state, is from Ekhart Tolle. The eternal Now is St. Thomas Aquinas' Nunc Stans, which is his term for eternity or God's time dimension, which is really out of time and out of place, but in another dimension that is unknowable by the conscious human mind. To enter into the Eternal Now, and enjoy the Oneness of Being, our Ego has to die over and over again. It doesn't go down easily. You have to drown it, choke it, starve it, squash it, humiliate it, beat it to death with a baseball bat, and it will still come back again tomorrow and try once more to destroy your peace of soul, and ruin your life in the next moment in the precious and powerful NOW.

We are talking here about human Ego that has taken about 400,000 years to evolve in our 'survival of the fittest' brains. We are bucking against very strong evolutionary instincts, but the daily practice of dying to Ego can be a transformative experience that changes our lives forever. The Dark Night of the Ego leads inevitably to a mystical experience of the Oneness of Being. If I lose my self-conscious Ego, I begin to experience a closeness to earth and to all visible and tangible reality. I am no longer conscious of separation from the world around me, or of my *self* as self, but of the *infinite self* of the universe. I become the Universe's self-consciousness.

Once you go through the agony of Ego suicide, truly letting go of your identity as a very special, unique individual human person, you enter the mystical experience of the Oneness of Being. Evolution produced each of us as unique human beings like snowflakes and fingerprints, and it's our job to embrace the fact that though we may be individuals materially speaking, we have to accept the fact that spiritually speaking, we are One with the divine element of the universe, the transcendent, yet paradoxically gravitational, power of Love that holds everything that exists together.

This is living without Ego: first we kill our Ego, and then we give ourselves to love. They are really two sides of the same coin. Tails we live without Ego; heads we live in love. Living without Ego *IS* living in Love. You have heard it all before: "Love your neighbor as yourself, " "Do unto others as you would have them do unto you." This is the mystical experience of the Oneness of being. Your body would still be encompassed by time, and your spirit/self would be bound to your body as a temporary "location" in space/time, if we can use a spatial term for a spirit. But you will be free from the pain-body that Ekhart Tolle describes. It is our Ego/ false self, containing all the memories, injuries, insults, traumas, anxieties, mistakes, and above all, losses, from your past life. Our entire human existence is organized, chaotically, around loss: loss of the security and comfort of the womb, loss of infantile omnipotence, loss of innocence, loss of magical fantasy, loss of virginity, loss of confidence in adults, in the government, in teachers, in peers. Above all, loss of love through rejection, loss of consumer goods, jobs, homes.

The Good News is that without Ego to constantly distract you from the present moment by obsessing about the past or the future, you can literally rest in peace. Without Ego, you can actually experience the joy of suffering. When things go dreadfully wrong in our life, the usual human trap that we all fall into is to ask "Why Me?" But if there is no *Ego* there, then there is no *Me* there, but only a *We*. Go ahead, ask "Why us?" What is the answer that you get?

CHAPTER VIII
DYING WITHOUT EGO

THE INTRODUCTION EXPLAINED why I need a third book to complete my Twin Towers Trilogy. The first book left the universe with an Ego-less, unconscious God, while the second book left us humans without Ego's either. So I owe the universe a serious explanation and plan for how to proceed from here without an Ego. The unconscious God is the easiest part of my explanation because the only consciousness that we can be aware of as humans is our own material consciousness, very much dependent on a material brain with neuron cells to picture everything with accompanying stereo sound. Whatever God is, he/she/it definitely does not have high definition video accompanied with stereo sound. So we have to settle for a divine awareness that we simply dub "unconscious" or "not human consciousness." Of course, this unconscious God in its utterly mysterious and unknowable way is the "Ground of Being." We either accept its existence on faith, or intuition, or existential commitment, or we reject it, and are reduced to the atheist's explanation for the universe, which requires infinitely more faith or existential commitment than I am able to muster. You ask, "What is the atheists' explanation?" I don't know, ask THEM! I deal with the God who never was and the God who always was in the first two chapters of this book.

Now, the second book proceeded to hack to death my poor, barely functional Ego, and after a very serious self-analysis in which I concluded that faith, or intuition or existential commitment demanded that I commit Ego suicide. I called it the "Dark Night of the Ego, " and invited the reader to commit the same Ego suicide. I tried to explain this more extensively in Chapter VI of this book: " The Dark Night of the Ego" which is the agony of realizing that your self whom you thought was a somebody is just a nobody, and simply an anonymous, unnamed part of the universe. In the previous Chapter VII, we talked about Living Without Ego, which is the same as living in love.

Of course, without Ego, we need a plan for living the rest of our lives, in a thoroughly satisfying, Ego-less way. Simply speaking, the death of my Ego means we are all one in the eternal Oneness of Being. It means that we are no longer individual human beings, and we have to love our neighbor, not because he is our brother, but because he is ME. He's the only thing I have to love. If love means anything at all, and it does, then Love is God, God is Love, and God is All in All. We have used this expression for two thousand years, from St. John, "God is love". But God is Love is not just an abstract, metaphysical symbol, but a concrete statement that God is You, and Me, loving each other in this present moment.

Now are you ready for "Dying without Ego"? As I said above, when I first wrote "The Day My Ego Died," I signed it to all readers: "You are already dead, and living in heaven, in God's eternal NOW, but you will not enjoy it until all of your Ego is dead." Everybody, of course, wanted to know exactly what this meant. How could we be in heaven now? And what does Ego suicide mean? So I had to go back to my tenth therapy *session* with God as my therapist, where I ask God, "now will you tell me what it means for ME to be free?"

From *The Day My Ego Died*

"Now will you tell me what it means for me to be free?

"It means that you are not afraid to die. It means that you understand that the world belongs to you already and you belong to the world. When you own the whole world, you cannot lose it. You are free to let it go. Fear not, it will come back to you."

"But if I am dead," I begged Her, "how can the world come back to me?"

"When you are dead, you have gone back to the world."

Nine years later, I now know what I was trying to say: that the new death I was talking about is the suicide of the Ego. When your Ego dies, you go back to the earth. Remember Jesus' teaching: 'The meek shall inherit the earth', and 'Happy are the poor in spirit, for the Kingdom of heaven belongs to them.'

To continue my tenth therapy session in *The Day My Ego Died* I plead with God, "I want to understand what you are saying. It sounds so good, intellectually, in my head, but emotionally, in my gut, it scares me. Dead means to not be alive, and that hurts somebody who is alive like me."

"It doesn't hurt somebody who is dead like ME, " God said.

"Can you properly be said to be dead?" I replied.

"Can you properly be said to be alive?" God asked.

"Wow! This is heavy", I said. "When I am alive, I'm not really alive, and when I am dead, I am not really dead?"

"Until you understand that there is no difference between life and death, you will never be free."

After I wrote this, my Goombah, Emmett Wolfe sent us an E-mail in which he stated that he went by a synagogue in Manhattan, and it had posted on its outside billboard this quote from Teilhard deChardin: " We are not human beings having a spiritual experience, but we are spiritual beings having a human experience." Immediately, I understood what God had told me during my tenth session. There is no difference between life and death if we understand that we are spiritual beings who always were, are now, and always will be.

I again quote John Chuchman:

"The Real Good News we should be spreading is that "We do not need to be saved from anything other than a belief "That we are solely human.

"We were already saved when we were born, saved from nothingness.

"That is the only salvation that we will ever need."

The mystics among us: Jesus of Nazareth, Francis of Assisi, John Chuchman, Teilhard deChardin, and all, are telling us the same thing. There is no difference between life and death once our Ego is dead. St. Francis said, "It is in dying that we are born to eternal life." While Jesus said that "Anyone who believes in me, already has eternal life." And we can now say that by being born human, we enter consciously and unconsciously into eternal life. Believing in Jesus is one way to accomplish this, but any religion or philosophy or common sense or culture that teaches us the Golden Rule to do unto others as we would have them do unto us will bring us down the same way or "Dao". Karen Armstrong's new work on Compassion and the Golden Rule makes all of this crystal clear. Intuitively, we all understand that whatever we do unto others we are automatically doing to ourselves. We also understand that homicide is suicide, because if I and my neighbor are One, then I am killing myself when I kill my neighbor.

To go back to the tenth session on the death of Ego, "There is no difference between life and death?" I repeated. "But isn't that what Buddhism has been teaching for centuries?"

God answers, "You got it!" They call it 'nirvana': the final freeing of the soul from all that enslaves it. Through enlightenment, one gives up all passions, all hatreds, all delusions, all expectations of oneself or of others, and slips into the primordial sea of the womb, with no self-conscious ego, with no desires, and no fears."

Sal answers, "Talk about going home! You are saying that it's all about going back into the womb? But the fetus is not free. The fetus is trapped in solitary confinement like a prisoner." God says, "The fetus is free, because it is unborn and open to all possibilities: whether life or death or just existence. The fetus is free because it has an illusion of omnipotence."

When I wrote this nine years ago I had no idea what it meant. But the poet John Chuchman whom I quoted above recently explained it by his poetic statement, called "The Real Good News," that " we do not need to be saved from anything other than a belief that we are solely human. We were already saved when we were born, saved from nothingness. That is the Only Salvation we will ever need." In my way of seeing it, the new born infant assumes that it IS the whole universe. It has absolutely no Ego, and therefore identifies with the Oneness of Being. It has no self-awareness, no sense of separation from the rest of reality. The Universal Spirit Who gives life, being, substance to all Being is born in each human being. The Buddhists and the Hindus call this re-incarnation or the transmigration of souls. Human 'survival of the fittest' instinct drives the individual human person to become an Ego, and compete with the rest of the Universal Spirit's emanations, instead of becoming One with them in mutual concern. Buddha's best teaching is to live without any expectations of oneself or of others. The ultimate transmigration of soul: God, the One Spirit/Soul of the universe becomes incarnate in all of the universe. Each human being becomes the self-consciousness of the universe. This is not an end-point in some future. This is happening right now in temporal time and in the One Eternal Now, as it was in the beginning, is Now, and ever shall be.

CHAPTER IX
HOW TO PRACTICE DYING

THE OLDEST CLICHÉ' in New York City is "How do you get to Carnegie Hall?" "Practise, practise, practice." In my High School Seminary, the first thing we learned from our German Professor, Charlie Fehrenbach, was "Ubung macht den Meister," "Practice makes perfect." Wouldn't this apply to dying more than to any other activity in life? Notice I said 'life.' Death should be our last and noblest act of life. Death should not be a mere acceptance of the inevitable but our finest hour. Death is going home: going to our parents' house for a White Christmas, going to our Grandparents' house for a New England Thanksgiving. Death should be our final grand-slam walk-off home run. We should all come down to earth as winners.

At the beginning of "The Day My Ego Died", I quote Teilhard DeChardin, in Christianity and Evolution, where he says, " If, as a result of some interior revolution, I were to lose in succession my faith in Christ, my faith in a personal God, and my faith in spirit, I feel that I should continue to believe invincibly in the world. The world (it's value, its infallibility, and its goodness)—that, when all is said and done, is the first, the last, and the only thing in which I believe. It is by this faith that I live, and it is to this faith, I feel, that at the moment of death, rising above all doubts, I shall surrender myself."

It seems that Teilhard meditated for many years on this theme of faith in a personal God, and in Christ, and in spirit itself, and he faces death, as I do, as a home coming to earth. This is a dedicated Jesuit priest and anthropologist, who remained faithful to his religious vows until death, even though he was silenced by Rome and forbidden to write or teach anymore in a Catholic University. So he went to China to continue his work in paleontology and evolution. One morning, as the sun rose, he said Mass by holding up his hands to embrace the globe of the rising sun, and pronounced the sacred words of consecration over the universe of evolution, saying: "This is my body!" The universe, the world, as Teilhard calls it is the Body of the Great Spirit! In dying, we go back to the earth we came from.

So how do we practice dying, whether it is death of Ego, or death of Body. Every day we have marvelous opportunities to practice dying. If I were a stand-up comedian like my favorite, George Carlin, I would say that comedians practice dying every time they get in front of an audience. George had so much practice dying that it must have been a piece of cake for him to actually die. George would probably say that you either kill the audience or be killed by them. Every crowd is such a tough crowd that if you don't kill 'em, YOU'RE GONNA DIE! For the rest of us mortals, we have to grasp the chances that befall us every day, especially as we move into the Super Senior Golden Age. I'll give you a concrete example.

One morning, recently, I was awakened at 6:20 by a phone call asking me what happened. Three golfers were waiting for me to tee off at 6:52. It was a nightmare that I have had dozens of times, only this time it was not a nightmare, it was really happening. You see, I was slated to play in the semi-finals of the Governor's Cup matches at the Salisbury Senior Golf Club. It was the first time in about five years that I had qualified for the match play at our club. I was excited all week preparing for my last shining moment with the club, since we will be moving to Florida for good at the end of this season. So now, as I am answering this phone call from the starter's booth at the golf course, my special golf alarm clock was going off. It's a little fat golfer with a yellow mustache and a green tam-o-shanter that my friends, the Healy's gave me for Christmas, and the little fatty is crying out to the sound of birds chirping: "Wake up! Wake up! You're going to miss your tee time!" And then there is the swish of a golf-swing and a splash of a ball hitting water. The alarm clock keeps repeating this annoying and gruesome taunt until you push down the button on his freaking green tam-o-shanter.

Between answering the phone and pushing down the button, I suddenly realize I had set the alarm one hour late. I told my opponent to wait for me, and I would be there in 20 minutes, which would have been in time to tee off at 6:52. Except I didn't get to the golf course till 7:00 and the threesome had gone without me!!

Now, I have been claiming for 10 years that my Ego is dead, and nobody, especially my wife and best friends, believes that. So, I will let you, kind reader, decide. I swear I was not very upset by this senior moment catastrophe, because I immediately recognized it as a perfect opportunity to practice Ego suicide and dying to self which is, after all, the only preparation for death that we really need. Each time that we die to our Ego makes the ultimate death of our body a little bit easier.

When I ran to the starter's station and asked what happened and he told me they took off without me, I could have gone into an Ego rage. Why did they call me and wake me up and rent a golf cart for me with my opponent if they did not intend to wait for me, which is done all the time in our club? I thought that, but I did not allow it to upset me. It was simply my mistake, my senior moment. It's my job to accept my human condition, accept my vulnerability to imperfection, and move on to the next adventure in life and death. It's not my job to question what other people should or should not have done. It doesn't matter what I would have done if I had been in their place. Next time, set the alarm clock correctly, which I have done. Not only that, but I set a second alarm clock just to be sure. I'm not dead yet, but I'm practicing.

This senior moment of completely mixing up 5:00 AM with 6:00AM is what dying is about. It's a loss of control of our most critical faculties: attention and concentration, the Ego's biggest defenses after denial and projection. Ego doesn't want to die. Even though Ego is a mental construct of the brain and only exists as an idea of the brain, it functions as the Chief Executive Officer of the body and commands the body in all matters of life and death. It seems to me to be a product of evolution and the survival of the fittest. The Ego that best survives the opposition passes on its body's genes by the process of natural selection. The Ego is mortified, which literally means, put to death, by lapses in concentration. That is why we humans have so many wars and greedy dominators.

But whether we are rich or poor, oppressors or the oppressed, we better learn how to die to Ego, or we are looking at some very ugly deaths. Not only, but if we really understand that we are already dead, and living in God's ETERNAL NOW end time, we cannot enjoy it unless our Ego dies.

St. Alphonsus Liguori, founder of the Redemptorist Congregation of which I was a member for 30 years, was famous for his insistence on preparation for death. His best known book, by that name, was written at his desk with a real human skull as a reminder.

In the seminary, they often told us the story of St. Aloysius Gonzaga who was the patron saint of seminarians. Aloysius was enjoying recreation one day playing bocce, and St. Ignatius Loyola came up to him and asked him, "Aloysius, if you knew you were going to die this day, what would you do?" The seminarian simply replied, " I would just go on playing bocce." Is death that big a deal, if the in-house bocce championship is at stake? Especially if you are at peace with God and man, and time and eternity?

But the best illustration of my thesis on preparation for death I received from a lecture by Dr. John Yankovitch at our local Molloy College on the Code of the Samurai. The central point in the selection of Samurai warriors was the readiness to die at any moment for his master. Since every moment could very well be the moment of death, the Samurai had to decide whether he was ready to die every moment at the command of his master. If there was the slightest hesitation, the candidate would not be accepted into this elite culture of death. The Kamikaze of World War II fame (or infamy) came out of that culture. The nuclear engineers who are now working at the tsunami dismantled nuclear plant in Japan are from that same culture. Perhaps they learned it from the honey bees who designate certain worker bees to stand guard at the entrance to the hive and sacrifice their lives by stinging any foreign insects that try to invade the hive. All bees, of course, die when they sting someone or something, because they leave the major part of their intestines in the one they sting.

In these ten years since 9/11/2001, there has been a great deal of talk and writing about suicide bombing. Is it a crazy Muslim fanaticism, to go against our primary instinct for survival by a sublimation, as Freud would call it, desperately seeking a Paradise of 73 Virgins? I am sure Freud would have loved the suppressed sexual connotation. If it is such a gruesome death looking for such a sensual reward, I wonder what the female jihadist martyrs are killing themselves for? To become one of the 73 Virgins for some "fellow" martyr?

But my own opinion vis a vis suicide bombers and Samurai swordsmen is that all war is suicidal, always was and always will be. If you do not think the Phalanxes of Alexander and the Roman Legions of Julius Caesar were suicidal, think again. If you don't think the charge of the Light Brigade in the Crimean War, and Pickett's charge at Gettysburg was suicide, think again. The greatest delusion foisted on men and women at arms is the cynical and selfish statement of their commanders that they must fight to take care of each other and come back home alive. This is an unconscious recipe for death rather than a proper preparation for death. The Japanese Samurai are much more honest. We're sending you to die. Are you ready? On your mark, get set, go!

I could go on and write about war as suicide and how the survival of this planet and of this race is severely threatened by our 10,000 year history of constant war. But I leave that theme to better minds than mine to develop. The daily practice of dying is my theme.

In attending Professor Yankovitch's lecture on the Code of the Samurai, I noted to him that we should all be ready to die at any moment, because we well could die at any moment. Going further, I said that if you subscribe to the philosophy of the Oneness of Being and the "Power of Now," and therefore to the Oneness of this eternal moment, now, then every moment is precisely your moment of death. Each moment of time, we die all over again. If the only reality is NOW, once this moment is over, we are dead as doornails and have to be re-born in the next moment. It sounds too dizzy and scary when you say it, but it's true.

With all this practice at dying, our final death of body moment should become as familiar as our most comfortable pair of shoes. I am sorry I cannot help you with the moment after the death of the body. For that moment, you will have to go to the Christian tradition of resurrection, and the best reference I know on that is Bishop John Shelby Spong, who is fast becoming the world-wide leader of Progressive Christianity. A series of lectures he gave at Harvard Divinity in 2001 led to *"A New Christianity For a New World:* Why Traditional Faith Is Dying and How a New Faith Is Being Born." Many exciting new insights into the meaning of resurrection have been propagated these last few years. For Spong, the stories in the New Testament about the resurrection of Jesus were all allegories and metaphors used by the first followers of Jesus for their own awareness of Jesus among them after his death. The resurrection to them meant that all of us, somehow, are going to be alive in some new way after the death of our bodies.

As far as I am concerned, the moment after the death of our body is going to be like the present moment in which you quietly experience unconsciously and intuitively, your Oneness of Being with Ultimate Reality. That is why you have to practice it now. Every time I see a tree, or a flower, or a blue ski, or a cloud, I practice becoming One with them. Sometimes I get carried away, so it is good to set up special times for meditation on the Oneness of Being, where you blot out all thought and simply behold with your inner sight, eyes half-closed, the World in which you live, and move, and have your Being. Try it now, and don't forget to breathe deeply, in fact follow your breath, both in and out.

This is the best I can do to explain a "Spirituality for the Age of Terrorism". My idea of God said to me 10 years ago: "Until you understand that there is no difference between life and death, you will never be free. " Also, Jesus says in St. John, "He who believes in Me already has eternal life." Your Ego likes to think that you are alive, not only now, but you will somehow live forever. Your Ego is engaging in wishful thinking. First of all, your Ego is a psychological construct, just like the Mechanisms of Defense of the Ego, such as Denial and Projection. You would have to study Ego psychology to totally grasp what this means. For now, you will just have to trust me that Ego is made up by each of us as a survival mechanism in this cruel world of survival of the fittest. The purpose of the Ego construct that is beat into us by parents, teachers, clergy, government, and society, is our survival as individuals. Without a strong set of Ego defenses, a nervous, neurotic superego to control our Id, or instinctual impulses, the individual will not survive into adulthood. But as we mature into adulthood, we have to gradually understand that our Ego is fighting hard against our best interests, especially against our destiny to lose self and fuse with the rest of reality in the Oneness of Being. That is precisely why we have to kill our Ego, not when our body dies, but right now. Don't be afraid, I assure you it takes quite a while to kill all Ego. The good news is: when the Ego finally dies, it is very easy for the body to let go and take the natural route to dissolution which is its destiny. And just as we have to commit Ego-suicide, we have to carefully monitor our body to decide, while we are still *compos mentis i.e in control of our own mind,* when the quality of life of the body decides when it needs to be terminated. Now I know the traditional teaching of most religions and cultures condemns the killing of both the Ego and the body to which it pretends to be the CEO. But I also hold this truth to be self-evident that we are not only endowed with the right to life, liberty, and the pursuit of happiness, but also with the right to terminate our bodily life if it is incompatible with liberty and the pursuit of happiness. In other words, we have the right to die. Does that mean that I endorse assisted suicide? Yes, with all the proper legal and spiritual safeguards, like expert medical, psychological, and spiritual counseling. Do I endorse euthanasia? Yes, with all the above precautions, with the emphasis on legal clearance through living wills, and "do not resuscitate", and "do not use any extraordinary means" clauses. When my older brother was brought from his nursing home to Massachusetts General Hospital two years ago, he was kept alive by literally shoving the breathing tube of a resuscitator down his windpipe. He was in agony, and the doctors could not remove the tube because he had cancelled his "do not resuscitate" living will. Since I was named as his proxy, the doctors asked me what to do. I said, "Remove the tube, and let's ask him." They removed the tube, and my brother shouted louder that I had heard him speak in years, "Do not let them put that down my throat. This was the worst pain I ever felt!" I said to the doctors,

"You heard him." My brother passed away about four hours later. Now I know this is not the same as assisted dying or euthanasia, but the same principles and rights and responsibilities apply.

It is extremely important that these decisions be made long in advance so that the dying person is well-prepared for death while he or she is still able to make decisions for himself or herself. At the first sign of terminal illness, the patient should be offered a serious course of counseling in which he is apprised of all his rights and responsibilities. But hopefully, by practicing the death of Ego you will be ready for death of the body without counseling. For my Golden Age brothers and sisters I offer this Twin Towers Trilogy as a basis for the Spirituality of Dying. I have long been suggesting to patients, relatives, and friends that they attend some kind of "Preparation For Death Retreat," in which we prepare our own funerals, not just pre-pay the burial services, but more importantly, compose our own personal wake and memorial services, along with the music and readings, and any requests we have for speakers, eulogists, or performers. Why not, since it is your last performance, in the flesh, so to speak.

Personally, I would like to have one dancer do "Zorba the Greek" for me. If we could get somebody to get up and lead all assembled in the Zorba dance that I did on Better World Retreats, that would be really neat. Of course, I would rather do it myself as a kind of pre-funeral performance, but probably, if I am not already dead, it will kill me for sure, but only my body, because my Ego will already be dead.

(I hope.)

CONCLUSION

I MIGHT CALL THE Conclusion of my Trilogy on the Twin Towers: *God and Man in Nemo Land*, (Nemo being the Latin word for No One.) So the thesis of my three books is that God is No One, and Man is No One. In a sense, this third and last book is a self-analysis, just as the first two books were. In the first book, I picture God as the patient, and myself as the therapist, while in the second book I picture God as the therapist, and myself as the patient. In both books, I am really analyzing myself. In the first, I am analyzing my ideas about God, while in the second; I am analyzing my ideas about myself. Thus, the third book became a straight and direct analysis of who I am, and what I am, as I continue to live it up before the grim reaper comes to scythe me down. Actually, this last analysis turned out to be more about who I am not, rather than who I am.

Like Moses on Mt. Sinai, I would love to cop-out like the Hebrew author of long ago, and simply say, as he has God say, " I'm Me!" But I'm not God (at least not in that old way,) so I owe the anxious reader a longer answer. I am not Me, in the sense of Me as another word for Ego. I am definitely not my Ego, as I have been trained to be all my life. I am Nemo, that is, No One, and at the same time I'm everyone. In fact, I'm you. Once you accept the Oneness of Being, you see the human task as that of voluntarily giving up the search for a unique identity and individuality, and accepting somethingness as our final salvation. As my friend John Chuchman writes, by merely being born we are saved from nothingness:

The Real Good News
We should be spreading
        Is that
We do not need to be Saved
        From anything
Other than a belief
That we are solely human.
We were already Saved when we were
born, Saved from nothingness.
That is the Only Salvation We will ever need,
Except perhaps from Fear.

I spent the first fifty years of my life searching for a personal God, asking questions about Him from anyone who would listen. May I ask one more question? Why are we always searching for God or waiting for Godot, as the Becket play calls him? Why can't we just accept that there is no more need to search if we have already been found by Ultimate Reality, or the Unmanifested? As the old song "Amazing Grace" says so beautifully, "I once was lost, but now I'm found, was blind, but now I see." As I quote Paul Tillich, the existential theologian, we need to acknowledge that "we have been grasped by the God above the God of Theism."

From *The Day My Ego Died* **pp.185**

"I will share a paper I wrote while undergoing my own mid-life crisis. It was on existential neurosis. I had discovered the existential theologian, Paul Tillich, who wrote *The Courage To Be.* **In it Tillich talks about the process of disillusionment that religious people go through when they have to give up their childish fantasies of a 'cosmic Papa', who is going to take care of us, and, of course, give meaning to our lives by rewarding good and punishing evil. According to my paper, we had to come to the realization that we had been using religion as a neurotic way of avoiding loneliness and anxiety, and, of course, dealing with death. Tillich says, " It is as atheistic to affirm the existence of God as it is to deny it. God is being itself, not** *A being.***" Tillich goes on to say that one must give up the God of theism in order to be grasped by the "God above the God of theism." In other words,**

Tillich affirms that the "Courage To Be" results from experiencing oneself as "being grasped by the power of Being itself."(*The Courage To Be, Paul Tillich, New Haven, Yale Press, 1953).* Very subtly the existential therapist helps his client to see that accepting the anxiety of non-being is a great courageous act of commitment to whatever being there is in our ability to accept the unacceptable: the meaninglessness of our lives! For many, this goes beyond words to explain. It is an intuitive insight that one can indeed accept acceptance by the transcendent power of Being that gives meaning to life.

"Dag Hammarskjold, the deceased Secretary General of the United Nations, has become a model of modern existential man and woman. He seems to have made this authentic commitment to self, mankind, and world. Shortly before he died he wrote in Markings, (Dag Hammarskjold, *Markings, tr. By Leif Sjoberg & W.H. Auden, NY, Knopf, 1964),* " I don't know Who or What put the question, I don't even remember answering, but at some moment I did answer *YES* to Someone or Something—and from that hour I was certain that existence is meaningful and therefore my life, in self-surrender, had a goal.

"All the elements are there for the ideal existentialist: an intuitive grasp of meaning, and commitment to a goal. But the paradox is even deeper when we read what Hammarskjold wrote just before his tragic death: " I came to a time and place where I realized that the Way leads to triumph which is a catastrophe, and to a catastrophe which is a triumph, that the price for committing one's life would be reproach, and the only elevation possible to man lies in the depths of humiliation."

"Now, after 25 years since I wrote those words, and quoted Tillich and Hammarskjold, it is very poignant to me what a Christ figure Dag Hammarskjold has turned out to be. In his words of catastrophe becoming triumph, and elevation lying in humiliation, we see the crucifixion and then resurrection of Christ that has come to be the paradigm of existential commitment for the ages.

"Little did I know that the horrific events of September 11 would be a watershed event that proved once and for all that the Ego God of theism was dead, and along with Him, my own Ego was doomed to die."

If, as Tillich says, it is atheistic to affirm the existence of a Personal God as most religious people do, then the atheists who deny the existence of God are denying the same God, the personal God whom I state in this book never really existed. The atheists themselves are constantly scoffing at religious people who are always talking to their "imaginary friend." But as for the God who always was, as I speak of in this book, the militant atheists are so busy fighting for the absence of god that they are blind to the presence of God everywhere. Is it really the absence of God or the absence of goodness and love of which they are so painfully aware? Atheists talk incessantly about the lack of love and goodness in people who profess to believe in God. Are atheists, therefore, implicitly affirming a longing for a benign spirit in the world? Do atheists wish they could be found by such a benign spirit as we existentialists? Perhaps not me, as part of the we, but perhaps Paul Tillich and Dag Hammarskjold?

I am happy to say that the "God who always was," turned out to be the universal Spirit, identical with the universe itself. He was no longer the Creator, but "Creation" itself. Since I now believe in the Oneness of Being, I have to affirm both Creator and Creation as One Being.

In fact, creation is an idea that comes first from the creation myths of all primitive peoples, until it becomes a thesis, or hypothesis, of Christian philosophy. The Christian philosophers had to postulate an "uncaused cause", an infinite "Prime Cause" for the existence of a finite universe. But who decided that the universe is finite? The latest scientific findings seem to point at an infinite universe. According to Karen Armstrong in *The Case For God,* the ancient philosophers believed that the universe was eternal, had no beginning and no end. But when the Christian philosophers of the first and second centuries came along, they believed in a God, a theistic God, who was there before time began, and created the universe out of nothing. (*Karen*

Armstrong,The CaseFor God, Alfred A. Knopf, NY, Toronto, 2009. Pp.104, 105

But what if the universe is eternal, that is, always was, and always will be? Is that harder to accept than to accept the necessity of "some higher power" who pre-existed the universe and "created it out of nothing"? This is not to deny the existence of God in the sense that I have described in "The God Who Always Was." This definitely not atheism, which says simply:"There is no God. We don't need a great, powerful being separate from the universe, because the universe *IS* what it is." The atheist's approach is very human, based on the Greek philosopher's definition of human as *a rational animal.* The rational animals who call themselves atheists do not need a creator. They see the universe through rational eyes and accept it for what it is. They also accept their animality for what it is: a material existence which arises out of matter and ceases to exist by returning to the *potentiality of matter* as the Greek philosophers put it. But the atheists, by fixating on reason and the intellect, are ignoring other aspects of humanity, especially what we call so glibly and easily *the human spirit.* What is the human spirit? What is the universal desire for immortality in one way or another? Is it the wishful thinking of the limited human intellect, knowing it is mortal and yet wishing to somehow live on? In the age of anxiety, coupled with the age of terrorism, of global climate change, of overpopulation, of the exhaustion of natural resources, especially of fossil fuels, of nuclear meltdown, of massive earthquakes and tsunamis, how does a 21st century human deal with death, whether it is his own death, or the deaths of countless others?

The Mystical Experience of Eternal Life

I ask for one last indulgence on the part of the reader who may be put off by my invitation to a mystical experience. I firmly believe that all human beings have mystical experiences all the time, but few are aware of what is happening to them. People have these deep poetic, or intuitive episodes, sometimes vey brief, sometimes very extended, in the woods, at the movies, in a museum, at the ocean, on a mountain, in a zoo, in a Church or Temple, on a skyscraper street, and almost endlessly. I was surest of a mystical experience when I first looked into the Grand Canyon at sunset on New Year's Day. I realized what awe was. I was unable to speak, but of course, words were totally irrelevant. Over the next two days, studying all the tourist signs, realizing that it took the Colorado River 2 million years to carve out that awesome canyon, over and over again I experienced without knowing it, the confluence of time and eternity.

What is behind such experiences? I have said above that man was defined by philosophers as *a rational animal*. But in a more playful mood, they also defined us as *risible animals*, that is, we are the only animals who can laugh. They had a lot of fun with this definition because humans are the only ones who can laugh because we can see the contradiction between time and eternity, and laugh uncontrollably at the humor of our situation. A purely rational animal would say that time cancels out eternity, and eternity cancels out time. But if you can laugh at the paradox that you are temporarily in this moment of time, and simultaneously in the eternal NOW of Forever, you just had a mystical experience.

The Buddhists call moments like this a "Buddha experience", because Buddha means "The Awakened One." These moments are also called "Enlightenment", because they feel like a sudden lamp goes on, and we see a blank screen without images or words, and know intuitively that there is nothing to say or think because we *ARE*, we taste existence in our inner self. We feel no need to explain what happened, especially to our self. We feel we could go for the rest of our life without ever saying a word again.

Why do all the mystics sing the same international anthem: "Everything is beautiful, in its own way." Every human, every tree, even pain is beautiful. There is a "terrible beauty" in suffering, sorrow, and chaos. The followers of Gautama Buddha, "the Awakened One", are the best at accepting suffering as the only school for learning compassion. The compassion of humans for each other and for the earth is the "terrible beauty" that makes life worth living, and makes dying worth doing. But just as Buddha has the best teaching on suffering, so Jesus has the best teaching on love. For Buddha, suffering is the key to compassion and ultimately entrance into *Nirvana*. For Jesus, love is the key to dying to Ego, and entrance into eternal life.

We can sum up all of Jesus' teaching by his simple words, "He who believes in me *HAS ETERNAL LIFE*. All of our lives we have been taught that we will enter eternal life *AFTER WE DIE*. But that is *NOT* what Jesus is saying. He promises us that we will have eternal life *now, before death, not after death*. But if we read John carefully we realize that death must be an existential decision on our part. We have to *CHOOSE* to die to our Ego, to our false, narcissistic selves. This is another way of saying we have to "love one another as I have loved you."

John in his Epistle says that anyone who fails to love can never have known God, because *God IS Love*. But after reading John's Gospel, we realize that God is love is not an abstract definition of divinity, but a concrete statement that God is You and Me loving each other, and living in God's time and place, which Thomas Aquinas calls *Nunc Stans*: the eternal NOW. So to know God is to experience love, and to experience love is to lose oneself in others. Or as St. Paul puts it in his own brand of mysticism: "It is no longer I that live, but Christ Jesus lives in me."

Yes, all the world awaits the *Now* that is already here. This new vision of God as the intersection of time and eternity, as the transcendent Oneness of Being is truly transformative. What if we could teach our children how to be transformed in this way through love? Of course, we have rites of passage—all religions and cultures have them: especially for entering into temporal life (birth) and entering into eternal life (death.) But these are usually rituals celebrating the entrance into a particular religious group and exit from the group into the eternal dimension.

I think that Ekhart Tolle, in his two books *The Power of Now,* and *A New Earth* explains perfectly the basics of this new transformation, that, to me, sums up the best of Christian mysticism, zen Buddhism, and existential theology. In *A New Earth, (pp.30 to 34)(Ekhart Tolle,A New Earth/ Awakening To Your Life's Purpose, A PLUME BOOK,NY, 2006)*, Tolle talks about his first "awakening" when he was a student in London, riding on the subway, and saw a woman, obviously mentally ill, who was talking loudly to herself, and he came to the realization that it is all the thinking in our heads, especially about hurts from the past that paralyze us and take us away from the only life we have: this present moment. Tolle realized that he did that, too, but it took him another year or so to understand how to live in the present moment and ignore the past that was over, and for now, ignore the future which will have its moment in the sun when it becomes the now.

So much for the power of Now—but is this precious *NOW* a moment in *time* or in *eternity?* Perhaps the moment is both in time and in eternity. The scholastic philosophers of the middle ages called God's time: *The Eternal Now*:in Latin: *Nunc Stans*, that is NOW STANDING FOREVER. Is it perpetual motion or perpetual stillness? "As it was in the beginning, is now and ever shall be, world without end. Amen." So be it. Let it be. What does this mean?

Is time, and, indeed, eternity, really only a figment of our imagination? A product of our self-consciousness? Doesn't evolution teach us that we, mankind, are the universe's consciousness of itself? We have evolved as the universe's self-consciousness. We are, in a sense, the soul of the universe, we are proxies for the Universal Spirit, the Ground of the Oneness of Being. So, if time is indeed a figment of our imagination, does this give us an actual conscious insight into the purpose and meaning of the universe? Is life pointing to the purpose of matter? Is consciousness pointing to the purpose of life? Is matter its own purpose of being? Is life its own purpose? What about Paul Tillich's "Courage To Be" in which he says that living a meaningless life is very meaningful, because living needs no purpose. Life itself is meaningful in itself. It needs no meaning beyond itself. That is the main tenet of existential philosophy, that we create our own meaning by embracing existence for all it is worth. It is thus our own responsibility to find joy in merely existing in this eternal moment. For everything that ever happened or ever will happen is happening Now in this One Eternal Moment.

I recently re-visited the Museum of Natural History in Manhattan. It makes a wonderful dual visit from the Twin Towers Memorial at Ground Zero to the Museum on Central Park West. I revisited the Hall of the Universe, the Big Bang Theatre, and the Heilbrunn Cosmic Pathway. In the latter, you walk out of a cinematic depiction of the Big Bang 13 Billion years ago in the Big Bang Theatre and into the Cosmic Pathway that walks you through the first moment of the Big Bang and down the billions of years through the creation of light, and then quasars, and then stars, and galaxies, the formation of the planets, then bacteria, and myriad further life forms. As I walked the Cosmic Pathway with my friends, I was overwhelmed by the realization that these billions of years are only a construct of the human mind, that in reality, the big bang is happening right now in this eternal moment, and who knows, always will be happening when my self-conscious mind is no longer around to think it is happening.

In conclusion, birth is the first act of human life, while death is the last and finest act. To die peacefully, hopefully, compassionately, lovingly, is the goal of human existence. I like to think that if we follow some of the prescriptions in this book for dying to our Ego/false self, then final death of the body will be as I described it above. We should die actively, not passively. We should not merely "accept" death as unavoidable. We should embrace death as our final moment of triumphal rebirth.

We should live each moment of human life as if it were our last moment of human life, as it well may be. The Japanese Samurai were taught to live each moment as if it is the moment of death. If they are not willing to die at every moment, they will not be accepted as Samurai, because they will be useless to their Lord and Master. It should be the same for each of us, for, indeed, each moment of life may be our moment of death.

I am an avid skier, and I have learned to look at every run on the mountain as if it were my last. I love skiing so much that I cannot possibly give it up, just as I love life so much that I cannot possibly give it up. But for the past few years, I have skied each run joyfully, positively embracing it as my last run ever. One run down the mountain becomes the only run I have ever made, and I enjoyed each run as if it were my last. Will I ever ski again? I don't know, and somehow, it doesn't matter.

We have to take the words of Scripture literally, that "we have not here a lasting dwelling place", because as Teilhard DeChardin says, "We are not just human beings having a spiritual experience, we are much more: spiritual beings having a human experience." The human experience, with it's false-self Ego and self-consciousness is only temporary. Our spirit/self always was and always will be. "As it was in the beginning, is now, and ever shall be, world without end. Amen."

EPILOGUE

"**R**EMEMBER MAN, THAT you are dust, and unto dust you shall return"

Was it worth it, just to live, and then to die?

Once upon a time, somewhere in the vast universe, really everywhere and nowhere at all, is a Spirit-Self. This Spirit-Self is you, it is me, it is all of us who ever were or will be. Spirit has no matter, no parts, it is undivided, limitless, and infinite. It is One, it is True, it is Good, it is Beautiful. We, the Spirit-Self, are here, we are now, we always were and always will be. There is no past, no future, only now. We are all dead, and we are all very much alive. We have a love for Being which is ourselves. In fact we *ARE* Love, and because we are Love, we are a thing of beauty forever.

John Keats wrote about us:

"A Thing of beauty is a joy forever; It's loveliness increases; it will never Pass into nothingness; but still will keep A bower quiet for us, and a sleep
Full of sweet dreams, and health and quiet breathing
Therefore on every morrow, are we wreathing
A flowery band to bind us to the earth."

Some of us are huge fans of Jesus because he convinces us that we are already living in eternal life. It is very exhilarating that the latest theologians like Bishop John Shelby Spong are now saying that the Resurrection of Jesus means not that Jesus went to heaven, but that he went back to earth where he came from. "He who believes in me, already has eternal life." " I have risen and am still with you." No other religion claims that. We can have eternal life right now, just as Jesus has eternal life right now, through his "resurrected presence" among those who love him. The rest of us will not have millions of believers and followers who will follow us down the centuries.

That is why it is so important to grasp the significance of the "eternal NOW." Eternity is *NOW*. Eternity always was and always will be. Eternity is not a lot of time before and after. Eternity is out of time, beyond time, beyond the material, beyond the moving parts of cosmic explosions. Eternity is Now and Forever.

Jesus went back to the earth where he came from, not back to a heaven he never came from. "He has gone before you into Galilee." Galilee is where Jesus came from: from the earth of Nazareth, And it is to the same earth that we shall all return—where we came from.

It is my consummate joy to be named *Umana* which means *Human in Italian and in Spanish*. Human, of course, comes from *humus* which means "soil." We humans are all of the soil. "Remember humans that you are soil, and unto soil you shall return."

I can't wait to go home to earth. Yes, Tom Wolfe, you can go home again, FOR EVER. The earliest followers of the crucified Jesus would sing in their liturgies: Maranatha, Amen, Come Lord Jesus.

> Now that I no longer exist as an Ego, where do *WE* go
> from here? Nowhere.

> We are already here. In fact, *WE ARE. FOREVER.*

THE END

BIBLIOGRAPHY

(Excluding all the Titles Mentioned in the Bibliographies of the First two books.)

Armstrong, Karen, The Case For God, Alfred

A. Knopf, NY, 2009

Armstrong, Karen, *The Great Transformation, The Beginning of our Religious Traditions, Alfred*

A. Knopf, NY, 2006

Armstrong, Karen, *A Short History of Myth*, Canongate, Edinburgh, 2005

Borg, Marcus J., *Jesus: Uncovering the Life, Teachings, and Relevance of a Religious Revolutionary*, Harper, San Francisco, 2006

Fox, Matthew, *Creation Spirituality: Liberating Gifts For the Peoples of the Earth*, HarperCollins, NY, 1991

Fox, Matthew, *A Spirituality Named Compassion*: Uniting Mystical Awareness With Social Justice, Inner Traditions, Rochester, VT, 1999

Haight, Roger, S.J., *Jesus, Symbol of God*, Orbis Books, Maryknoll, NY, 1999

Kersschott, Jan, *This Is It:* The Nature of Oneness, Watkins Publishing, London,2004

Morewood, Michael, *God Is Near, Trusting Our Faith*, Crosswood, NY, 2002

Spong, John Shelby, *Eternal Life: A New Vision: Beyond Religion, Beyond Theism, Beyond Heaven and Hell,* Harper SanFrancisco, 2009

Spong, John Shelby, *Jesus For the Non-Religious*:Recovering the Divine At the Heart of the Human,HarperSanFrancisco, 2007

Spong, John Shelby, *The Sins of Scripture, Exposing the Bible's Texts of Hate to Reveal the God of Love,* HarperSanFrancisco, 2005

Teilhard in the 21st Century:The Emerging Spirit of Earth, edited by Arthur Fabel and Donald St.John, Orbis Books,Maryknoll, NY 2003

Tolle, Ekhart, *A New Earth: Awakening To Life's Purpose*, A Plume Book, NY, 2005

Tolle, Ekhart, *Practising the Power of* Now: *Essential Teachings, Meditations, and Exercises From The Power of Now, New World Library, Novato, CA 2001*

Wright, Robert, *The Evolution of God*, Little Brown, NY,2009

* 9 7 8 6 2 1 4 3 4 0 4 5 3 *